Eva Wincent &
Paula Hammerskog

Oodles of Crochet

Trafalgar Square
North Pomfret, Vermont

Preface

Learning how to crochet is one of the easiest things to do. All you need is some yarn, a crochet hook, and good instructions. You can start with chain stitches and single and half double crochet. That will get you well on the way. After that, you can learn for the rest of your life.

The two of us who wrote this book have different perspectives on crochet. Eva Wincent has crocheted for many years and will take on a coat or a prettily decorated towel. Paula Hammerskog uses crochet for relaxation between more advanced knitting projects or to embellish knitted or embroidered fabrics.

We wanted our book to be what we couldn't find in the shops—a book that both teaches the basics and develops crochet. We show you how to use various types of material for easy and fun ways of creating the most imaginative items and garments. Here are pillows, blankets, bags, shawls, sweaters, and, of course, a granny square or two.

Everything shown in the book has been crocheted with high quality yarn. Even if we use crochet for different projects, we have the same attitude towards quality. When we take the time for handcrafts, we want results that will be durable, not just pretty things to look at. Scarves and other garments should be washable, the bags filled up and used.

Eva Wincent & Paula Hammerskog

First published in the United States of America in 2014 by
Trafalgar Square Books
North Pomfret, Vermont 05053

Originally published in Swedish as *Virka mera.*

ISBN: 978-1-57076-685-5

Library of Congress Control Number: 2013923087

Translation by Carol Huebscher Rhoades
Crochet instructions and text: Eva Wincent, Paula Hammerskog
Photography: Rikard Westman
Graphic design: Lotta Axelsson

Printed in China

10 9 8 7 6 5 4 3 2 1

Contents

The Basic Building Blocks

There is really only one difficulty in crochet: keeping track of the number of stitches (= width) and rows (= length). Many people who crochet have also done some knitting, where the number of stitches is easy to control because you can simply count how many stitches are on the needle.

This is more complicated in crochet because you usually have only one stitch on the hook, and the rows vary in height depending on the type of stitches being used. At the end of this chapter, we will help you solve this problem and then you'll be ready to continue crocheting.

Almost all crochet projects begin with a common slip knot and then you work a number of chain stitches. These can be joined into a ring by linking the last chain stitch to the first. Crochet begun this way continues around from this central point. You can also turn after a certain number of chain stitches and crochet back. That will make a rectangular piece.

In this first chapter you'll find a number of different variations on the stitches, everything from slip stitches to treble crochet. Once you've learned how to do them, you can crochet whatever you like.

All of the instruction photos in the book are arranged for right-handed crocheters. If you are left-handed, see page 11 for tips on how to orient the pictures to the correct way for you.

Stitches

In this section, we'll show you, step by step, how to make a slip knot, chain stitch, single crochet, slip stitch, and, finally, various types of double crochet. This book uses the standard crochet terms from the United States. For British equivalents, see the abbreviations on page 26.

Single and double crochet stitches can both be worked as the first row above the beginning chain and later in the crocheted piece. Working them directly above a chain stitch begins by inserting the hook through the top loop of the chain stitch. When those stitches are worked later in the piece, the hook is inserted under both loops. Otherwise, they are worked the same way.

Most people don't usually work an entire piece in slip stitch because it grows so slowly in height. Slip stitches are, however, used to join a round, move the hook and yarn to another position in the crochet piece, and to join various sections.

SLIPKNOT

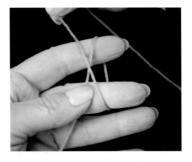 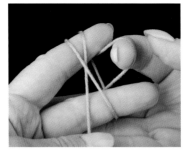 

1. Cross the yarn so it makes a loop, leaving a tail about 4 in / 10 cm long.

2. Bring the yarn through the loop with your right hand. Pull the yarn through and drop loop from left hand. The yarn has now formed a slip knot.

3. The slip knot is now complete and can be placed on the crochet hook.

CHAIN STITCH (ch)

1. Hold the yarn behind your index finger and catch it with the crochet hook. Catch the yarn so that it wraps around the hook from back to front. This is called a yarnover.

2. Pull the yarn through the stitch. Do not pull too hard because you have to be able to insert the hook into the stitch on the next row.

3. If you repeat steps 1 and 2, you'll have a line of chain stitches that you can work to desired length or a certain number of stitches.

SINGLE CROCHET (sc)

1. Insert the hook under either the top loop if you are working into a chain stitch…

…or through both loops if you have crocheted several rows. After this point, work the single crochet the same way.

2. Catch the yarn with the crochet hook and bring it through the stitch loop.

3. Now there should be 2 loops on the hook.

4. Wrap the yarn around the hook from back to front (yarnover).

5. Bring the yarn through both loops on the hook. The single crochet is now complete and you have one loop remaining on the hook.

SLIP STITCH (sl st)

1. Begin as for a single crochet and bring the yarn through the next stitch loop.

2. Pull the yarn through the stitch loop and the loop on the hook at the same time.

3. The slip stitch is now complete and you have one loop remaining on the hook.

HALF DOUBLE CROCHET (hdc)

1. Wrap the yarn around the hook from back to front (yarnover).

2. Insert the hook into the next stitch.

3. Bring the yarn through with the crochet hook and draw it through the stitch loop. Do not pull the yarn through the loops already on the hook.

4. There should now be 3 loops on the hook.

5. Wrap the yarn around the hook again (yarnover).

6. Pull the yarn through the 3 loops on the hook. The half double crochet is now complete and one loop remains on the hook.

DOUBLE CROCHET (dc)

1. Begin as for half double crochet (steps 1-4). There are now 3 loops on the hook. Wrap yarn around the hook (yarnover)…

2. … and bring yarn through two of the three loops on the hook. Two loops remain on the hook.

3. Yarnover again and pull yarn through the two remaining loops on the hook. The double crochet is now complete.

TREBLE CROCHET (tr)

1. Wrap yarn twice around the hook (2 yarnovers).

2. Insert the hook through the next stitch.

3. Use the hook to pull the yarn through the stitch but not through any of the loops on the hook. There should now be four loops on the hook.

4. Yarn over the hook and through two of the loops on the hook; three loops remain on the hook.

5. Yarn around the hook and through two loops. Two loops now remain on the hook. Finish by wrapping the yarn around the hook …

6. … and pulling it through the last two loops—now only one loop remains on the hook and the treble crochet stitch is complete.

TIPS FOR LEFT-HANDERS
If you are left-handed, you can use the same instructions by holding the pictures up to a mirror. That way, the illustrations will be shown as if crocheted by a left-handed person.

TURNING CHAIN STITCHES (tch)

Turning stitches are the extra stitches at the end of every row. Simply put, these are chain stitches worked onto the row so that the crochet hook will be at the correct height for the next row. The number of turning stitches depends on how the next row will be crocheted. A simple table listing how many turning stitches to make follows:

The next row is single crochet: 1 turning stitch
The next row is half double crochet: 2 turning stitches
The next row is double crochet: 3 turning stitches
The next row is treble crochet: 4–5 turning stitches

As a general rule, the turning stitches are counted as the first stitch of the new row, unless the turning is worked with a single chain stitch. That is not counted as a stitch. Most crochet patterns will specify whether or not the turning stitch(es) should be counted in the total stitch count.

In crochet instructions, the turning stitch is either given at the end of the row just completed or at the beginning of the row you'll crochet next. In practice, these are the same thing. Make the turning stitch rather loose so it will be easier to insert the hook into it. If there are several turning stitches, make only the top one a bit loose.

TIPS & TRICKS

When making double crochet stitches turned with 3 chain stitches, sometimes a hole develops between the turning chain and the first double crochet (because the first stitch is skipped). If that is the case, try turning with 2 rather than 3 chain stitches.

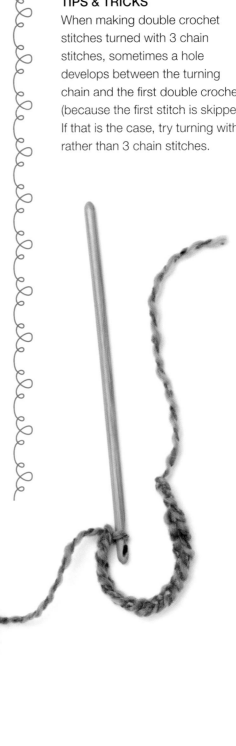

ENDING THE BEGINNING CHAIN

Almost all crochet begins with a slip knot and a specified number of chain stitches. If you want to crochet in the round, join the first and last chain stitches into a ring as shown in the pictures below.

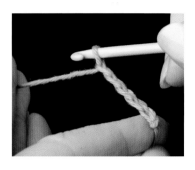

1. Make a slip knot and some chain stitches. The yarn to the left is the yarn coming from the ball of yarn.

2. When you have worked the specified number of chain stitches, insert the hook into the first chain stitch.

3. Make a slip stitch to join the chain into a ring.

Alternate method

If you want to crochet a circular piece without a hole at the center, work the stitches directly into the slip knot. You can pull the knot tight and avoid a hole. This method of beginning, sometimes called a "magic loop," is not as strong as beginning with chain stitches.

Wrap the yarn twice around your left index finger, insert the hook under the two wraps and catch the yarn. Make one or more chain stitches, depending on what type of stitches you want to crochet with (see table for turning chain stitches on the previous page) and continue crocheting around both wraps of the yarn for as many stitches as needed. Next, pull the yarn tight to close the hole. Finish with a slip stitch in the first chain stitch or in the top chain stitch if there are several.

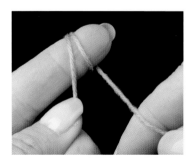

1. Wrap the yarn twice around your index finger.

2. Insert the hook under the yarn and catch it.

3. Work one or more chain stitches and some double crochet.

CROCHETING INTO DIFFERENT STITCH LOOPS

It is not very common to crochet into the front loops of the stitches on a large piece because it can be difficult to see if you are working into the front or both loops. If you are crocheting back and forth, there will be a stripe effect from crocheting into the front loops on every other row and in the back loops on alternate rows. If you crochet in the round, you can get the same effect by working only into the back loops.

When crocheting into the back loops, the crochet hook is inserted from the top.

Here's how to work into the front loops. Insert the hook from below.

Here's how to insert the hook into both loops of the next stitch.

Increases

You can increase at the beginning or end of a row as well as evenly across a row. The same technique is used whether the row is made of single crochet or some type of double crochet. These pictures show increases on a row of half double crochet.

If the increases are to be worked at the beginning of a row, work chain stitches to increase on the row below. If the increases are to be worked at the end of a row, work chain stitches on the same row. This increase can be made as long as needed. If the next row is one that needs turning stitches, these can be added to the chain.

INCREASING WITHIN A ROW

1. Work across in half double crochet to the stitch that will have an increase.

2. Work another half double crochet into the same stitch as the previous half double crochet.

3. The increase is now complete and the two stitches look like a V. You can increase several times on the same row.

INCREASING AT THE EDGES

1. Work the number of chain stitches that you want to increase at the end of a row. Don't forget to add any necessary turning chain stitches.

2. Turn the work and crochet into the chain stitches you just added.

3. Continue straight across the whole row. You can increase the same way on both sides but the increases won't be on the same row.

TIPS & TRICKS

You can also increase several stitches at each side of the same row. Remove the hook but leave the stitch loop open. With a new strand of yarn, work the specified number of chain stitches, join the new chain stitches to the saved loop, and cut new yarn. Continue straight across the whole row. Work following photos 1-3 above and end by working the new chain stitches.

Decreases

Decreases can also be made at the sides and within the row. The technique is similar to that for increasing. The same method is used for all types of stitches. Our photos show a row of half double crochet. Always work to the next-to-the-last step, when, normally, two loops remain on the hook.

DECREASING WITHIN A ROW

1. Work the first half double crochet to the last step when two loops remain on the hook.

2. Work the next stitch the same way—there should now be four loops on the hook.

3. Make a yarnover and pull the yarn through all the loops on the hook.

DECREASING AT THE EDGES

Decrease at the beginning of a row by working a slip stitch in each stitch of the previous row; each slip stitch = 1 decrease. Work the turning chain stitches and begin the next row.

To decrease at the end of a row, simply turn the work when the number of stitches to be decreased remains on the row. Work the turning chain and continue to the next row.

INCREASING AND DECREASING IN PATTERN

In principle, you increase and decrease in pattern the same way as we have described above, but it is likely that the increases and decreases must fit into a pattern structure. Compared to a lace pattern in knitting, it is easier to see where you are in the crochet pattern, and it is easier to continue to follow the pattern. To make a neat increase or decrease, you can increase or decrease in several steps and over several rows. If, for example, you are working a double crochet pattern with 2 dc, 1 ch, 2 dc, you can increase by working 3 dc instead of 2 at the beginning and end of the double crochet group. Decrease correspondingly by working 1 dc less at the outer edges of the group. Continue decreasing or increasing in steps until you have the correct number of stitches.

  If you need to eliminate several stitches you can work the same way as shown in the photos above. If you are working a pattern that widens a lot—for example, a fan pattern—you can crochet together one or a pair of stitches at the same time as you work slip stitches above them. Likewise, at the end of the row, work the same way instead of turning early.

Crocheting Around

Crocheting in the round is precisely what it sounds like—you simply work around and around without turning. The right side always faces you.

Usually you begin by working the specified number of chain stitches and joining them into a ring with a slip stitch into the first chain stitch. The first round is worked with all the stitches around the ring; that is, by catching the yarn around the ring instead of through a stitch. Begin the following rounds with the number of turning chain stitches needed for the stitches on that row. All the rounds end with the last stitch joined to the first with a slip stitch.

You will need to increase the total of stitches on each round by working increases evenly spaced around. If you group the increases, you can make other shapes, such as triangles, squares, hexagons, or octagons.

Here's an easy way to determine how many stitches you should increase around to make a flat circle. The number of stitches varies depending on which stitch you want to work with. "Tall" stitches such as double crochet need more increases around than shorter stitches like single crochet:

Single crochet = 6 sts per round
Half double crochet = 8 sts per round
Double crochet = 12 sts per round
Treble crochet = 24 sts per round

Continue increasing the same number of stitches on every round to the desired size. If you want a rounded circle, stagger the increases by a few stitches between the rows. If you want straight edges along each section, work new increases over previous decreases.

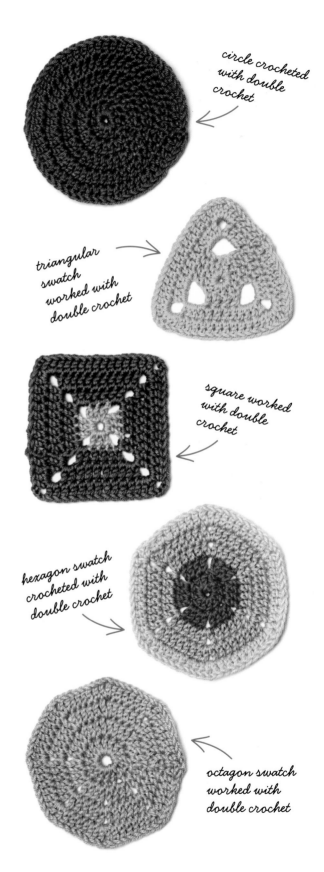

circle crocheted with double crochet

triangular swatch worked with double crochet

square worked with double crochet

hexagon swatch crocheted with double crochet

octagon swatch worked with double crochet

Crocheting Spirals

Begin as for working a circle, increasing around, but don't end with a slip stitch or begin the next round with a chain stitch. Simply continue around. You can crochet with single, half double, or double crochet, or in a pattern. Place a marker in the first stitch of the round so it will be easier to see where you need to increase. Increases should be made at the same rate as for crochet in the round.

The red spiral in the picture below is worked with double crochet but begins by tapering the height of the stitches with a couple of single crochet and then a couple half double crochet before continuing around with double crochet. If you want a smooth finish to the spiral, end as you began; that is, with 2 or 3 half double crochet and then a couple of single crochet stitches. End with a slip stitch; cut yarn and pull tail through the last stitch loop.

Cylinders

Begin by crocheting the base as large as you'd like, working either a circle or a spiral. Continue without increasing until cylinder is desired height.

Of course, you can make a cylinder without a base. In that case, make a row of chain stitches and join into a ring with a slip stitch and then crochet around or in a spiral. Take into consideration that the spiral easily twists. If you want a straight cylinder, either work around in rows or back and forth.

NOTE If you are working in single crochet, the beginning of the row will bias (slant) around, whether you work in a circle or spiral.

Cylinder 1 is worked with double crochet. The row change is staggered slightly to make a twisted "seam."

Cylinder 2 is worked back and forth in rows with double crochet. The seam is completely straight.

Cylinder 3 is worked as a spiral in single crochet. The shift between rows is invisible.

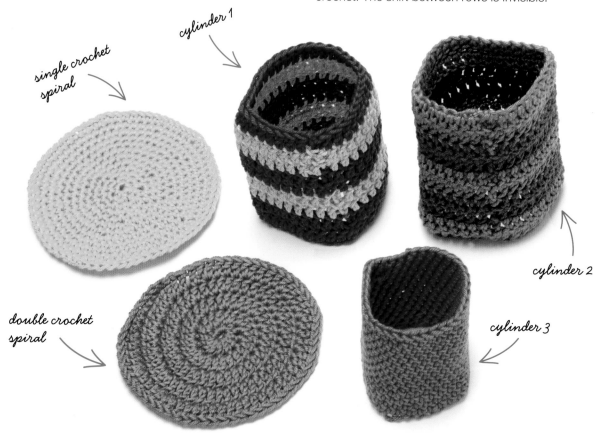

cylinder 1

single crochet spiral

double crochet spiral

cylinder 2

cylinder 3

Ovals

Make a row of chain stitches. Begin in the 2nd, 3rd, or 4th chain stitch, depending on whether you will work single, half double, or double crochet. First work down one side of the chain to the last stitch; work 3 sts in the last stitch and then crochet down the other side of the chain, ending with 3 sts in the last stitch; ch 1, join round with 1 slip stitch in the first or top chain st. Continue working around to desired size of oval, increasing at the short ends on every row so that the oval will stay flat. Place a marker at each short end and increase at the same rate as when crocheting around, but increase only at the short ends.

You can vary the shape by increasing more at one of the short ends to make one side wider, as for soles. You can make the piece rectangular by increasing with chain stitch loops at each short end and working around as for a granny square.

You can even vary the height of the stitches by beginning with a few single crochet, continuing with some half double crochet, and then working double crochet at the center; end to match the beginning. If you want a symmetrical shape, work the same way on the opposite side. This method is good for a leaf.

You can even use an oval as the base of a cylinder. In that case, crochet straight up without increasing.

Ovals are useful for making various shapes, such as toy animals or decorations like leaves or flowers. They also work well as bases for bags and foot soles.

Increasing in a Corner

Begin with a ring as for crocheting in the round. Make 1 or more chain sts depending on what type of stitch you are using; work 1 st, ch 1, 2 sts, 1 or more turning sts; turn. Now work 1 st more on each side of the chain st at the corner; the turning st is counted as a stitch. Continue until piece is desired size.

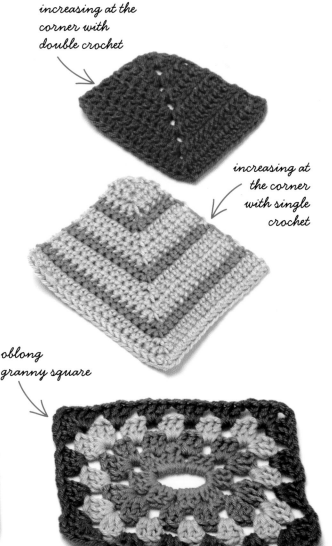

increasing at the corner with double crochet

increasing at the corner with single crochet

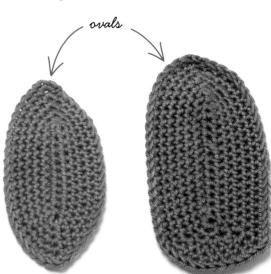

ovals

oblong granny square

Counting Stitches and Rows in Crochet

TIPS & TRICKS

Work chain stitches as evenly as possible. If they are very uneven, the first row will be harder to crochet because it will be difficult to see where the hook should be inserted. The chain might also twist easily so the hook sometimes goes into the right side and sometimes into the wrong side. The result will be an uneven first row. Depending on what you plan to crochet, it doesn't always matter. If the piece will be finished with an edging, then the beginning chain won't be visible.

It is not always important to make the exact number of chain stitches, but there should be a few more than needed. If you are working on a design without a written pattern, it isn't always easy to work out ahead of time the number of stitches that you'll need. Make as many chain stitches as you think you'll need *and* some extra. Rip out or cut away any extra stitches later but don't forget to leave a yarn end for finishing.

If you are going to work a lot of chain stitches to begin your piece, it's a good idea to keep track of the stitch count with markers. Place a marker on every 10th or 20th chain stitch.

The chain stitches will look like a V (some people describe them as a heart). Count each of the Vs and you'll count the correct number of stitches. Do not count the loop on the crochet hook.

The easiest way to count the number of stitches is to place a marker in the crochet. If it is important that the crochet be absolutely straight, you can baste in a marking thread on a blunt tapestry needle. Baste the thread in a couple of stitches from each side. Use the same technique when increasing or decreasing. If shaping the piece, be sure to weave in the thread further in from the sides. If you are going to decrease 18 times at each side, the marking thread should be at least 20 sts in from the side. A small but practical trick is to leave the thread in the needle so it can be held in place and you don't have keep threading the needle.

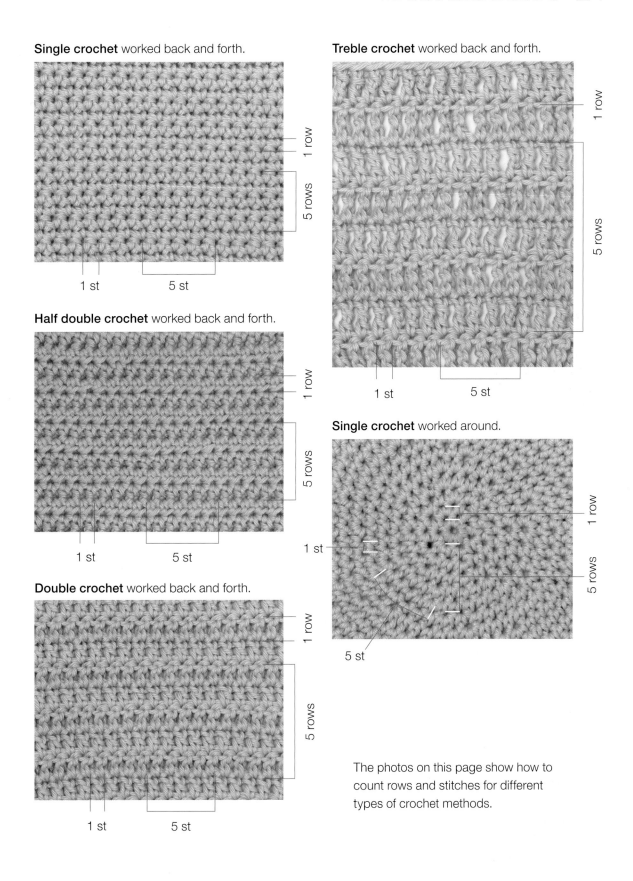

Single crochet worked back and forth.

1 row

5 rows

1 st   5 st

Half double crochet worked back and forth.

1 row

5 rows

1 st   5 st

Double crochet worked back and forth.

1 row

5 rows

1 st   5 st

Treble crochet worked back and forth.

1 row

5 rows

1 st   5 st

Single crochet worked around.

1 row

5 rows

1 st

5 st

The photos on this page show how to count rows and stitches for different types of crochet methods.

Reading a Pattern

Crochet patterns, precisely as for other handcraft instructions, are usually meticulously formulated. However, the difference between a crochet and a knitting pattern is obvious to anyone who does both of these crafts. If you are knitting, you are given an exact number of stitches to use and it is easy to know if you are working correctly or not. Crochet works differently.

When crocheting, you usually have a stitch on the hook and also have to count the number of double crochet stitches, chain stitches, or whatever stitch you are crocheting on every row to know if you are working correctly or not. Once you start crocheting, you'll quickly learn how to count stitches so you can turn after the correct number of stitches and keep the rows even.

Crochet instructions often consist of many abbreviations and sometimes charts. You'll find a list of the most common abbreviations in this chapter. Modern crochet patterns usually explain the abbreviations used in the instructions.

There are also crochet patterns with symbols for the different types of stitches. These should also be explained in a commercial pattern. The symbols can vary in different countries and traditions. Some countries use only symbols and codes and have minimal text. If you understand the symbols, you can work a Japanese or Thai crochet pattern even you don't understand a word of the text. We don't use any symbols in this book, just abbreviations, so we haven't included a complete list of crochet symbols.

YARN

All patterns are designed for a specific type of yarn, which is listed at the beginning of the instructions. You can substitute other yarns, but if you want a similar result to the original, you must choose a yarn as close as possible to the suggested yarn. If, for example, you substitute cotton for wool, the look and quality will be different even if the yarns are the same thickness. Make sure your gauge is correct (see below). Read more about yarn on pages 30-33.

GAUGE

The gauge describes how many stitches the yarn makes in a certain area (usually 4 x 4 in / 10 x 10 cm). If you crochet more loosely than the given gauge and also have fewer stitches and rows in 4 in / 10 cm, you should change to a smaller size hook. If you crochet more tightly, change to a larger hook. If you do not have the correct gauge, the size and even the shape of the piece you are crocheting will be different.

CROCHET HOOKS

Use the same size crochet as specified in the pattern, unless you need to choose a different size because you usually crochet very tightly or loosely. Go up or down a hook size until you find one that gives you the correct gauge.

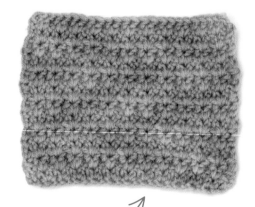

too tightly crocheted

crocheted just right

too loosely crocheted

Symbols & Abbreviations

Here are some symbols often used in crochet patterns; on the following page, you'll find a list of abbreviations. Sometimes several abbreviations are used for the same thing. The abbreviations are listed in alphabetical order.

* **   Asterisks are often used to indicate that something new is about to happen or to show that something should be repeated. Repeat the steps between the asterisks the specified number of times.

( ) [ ]   Repeat the steps between parentheses or brackets the specified number of times.

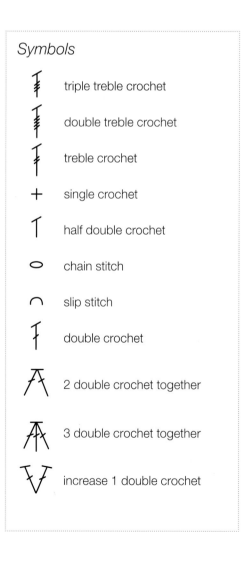

Symbols

	triple treble crochet
	double treble crochet
	treble crochet
+	single crochet
	half double crochet
o	chain stitch
∩	slip stitch
	double crochet
	2 double crochet together
	3 double crochet together
	increase 1 double crochet

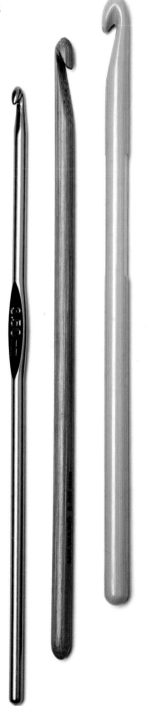

U.S. and British Crochet Abbreviations

There are many U.S. and British crochet terms in common but also some important differences. Unless otherwise noted in the column for British crochet terms, the abbreviations and meanings are the same for both traditions.

American Abbreviation	Meaning	British Abbreviation	Meaning
approx.	approximately	appr	
beg ch	beginning chain (chain at beginning of a row, usually substitutes for a stitch)		
BPdc	back post double crochet	tr/rb	raised back treble
ch	chain		
cm	centimeter(s)		
cont	continue		
dc	double crochet	tr	treble
dec	decrease		
dtr	double treble	ttr	triple treble
FPdc	front post double crochet	tr/rf	raised front treble
gr	group		
hdc	half double crochet	htr	half treble
in	inch(es)		
inc	increase		
lp(s)	loop(s)		
mm	millimeter(s)		
P	picot		
prev	previous		
quadtr	triple treble, long treble	trtr	quadruple treble
rem	remain(s) (ing)		
RS (rst)	right side (facing)		
rep	repeat		
sc	single crochet	dc	double crochet
sp	space		
sl st	slip stitch	ss	slip st
tch	turning chain		
tog	together		
tr	treble	dtr	double treble
tr/b	tr in back loop	dc/b	
tr/f	tr in front loop	dc/f	
W (WS, wst)	wrong side facing		
yd(s)	yard(s)		
yo(h)	yarn over (hook)		

Miscellaneous Terms

skip		miss
gauge		tension
afghan stitch		tunisian stitch

Terms

A number of terms and expressions are common in crochet instructions. Some of them need an explanation.

Generally, you begin crochet with a number of *chain stitches*. This can be described several ways, as, for example, *crochet x number* or *make x number of chain stitches*.

After the chain stitches have been made, it's time to begin the first row. It usually says to *insert the crochet hook* or *begin in the 2nd or 3rd* or another stitch. The stitches are always counted from the hook unless you are crocheting around. In that case, the chain stitches are formed into a ring by joining the first and last chain stitches together with a slip stitch. Even here, there are different ways to express the action, such as *join, end, crochet together,* or *join into a ring.*

Yarnover is a term that appears often. Yarnover, abbreviated as yo, indicates that the yarn should wrap around the hook in conjunction with making a stitch. Double crochet stitches are worked in several steps and, at each step, the yarn is caught and wrapped around the hook with one or more yarnovers.

Insert (or work) into is a term that needs some clarification. In this case, it refers more precisely to how or where the hook is inserted into the stitch or the row. For example, you can work into the front loop, which means that you insert the hook into the front loop of a stitch and crochet into it.

In crochet instructions, there are various ways of expressing how to work the stitches on, for example, the armhole, neck, and shoulders. This is easier in knitting patterns, because you can bind off and decrease stitches to the correct number. There is no bind-off in crochet. Instead,

This picot is crocheted as described in the text below with 3 single crochet stitches between each picot.

This variation is crocheted the same way as above, but the last chain is joined to the first chain with a slip st. This makes the points a bit higher.

it usually says to *eliminate stitches, leave stitches unworked* or to *crochet a certain number of stitches and then turn.* In practice, all these are the same thing—you turn after the correct number of stitches has been worked. At the beginning of a row, work slip stitches over the stitches that are to be eliminated.

In regards to decreasing, you can crochet 1 or 2 stitches together as in *decreasing* for knitting.

Picots are a common embellishment in crochet but they aren't always described. A picot is a little point, usually made by crocheting to the stitch where the picot will be placed, chaining 3, and then working as usual in the next stitch of the row. See photos above.

Materials, Equipment, & Preparations

A crochet hook, yarn (or whatever you've chosen for materials), measuring tape, and scissors—together with various types of needles for sewing together the pieces. This is really all you need, for the most part, to be able to crochet anything you want.

There are many different types of yarns and materials suitable for crocheting. What you choose depends, of course, on what you want to crochet. Loosely plied yarn produces a much softer result than tightly plied yarn, although the loosely plied yarn often results in a more uneven fabric.

Really uneven yarns or yarns with bubbles, eyelets, or fringe create a very exciting impression. However, it can be quite difficult to crochet with these yarns because it is much more difficult to differentiate the stitches than normal. If, for example, you crochet with a bouclé yarn, the hook often catches in the loops and you can't crochet quickly and smoothly.

Crocheting with leather, plastic, or fabric strips is popular. Thin leather or skin cords are available in many colors and are a fantastic material for crocheting everything from kindling baskets to vests. Plastic ribbon has come back and works well for trendy drapes or rugs; fabric strips make sturdy rugs or blankets. The fabric strips are easily made from old sheets and clothing; simply cut and rip them as for rag rug strips.

Yarn—Types and Qualities

Even if it is nice to crochet with many different types of materials, yarn is the most common. The choice of yarn is important—a well-crocheted project can quickly lose its shape if the yarn is bad quality. If you choose a high quality yarn, the result will be prettier and more durable. Cheap yarns are seldom high quality but a high price is not always a guarantee for high quality. Fashion yarns and yarns with special effects can sometimes be expensive without being particularly good.

If you crochet following a pattern, it is easiest to choose the yarn recommended in the pattern. If you substitute the yarn, be careful to choose a yarn with similar gauge, and don't forget to crochet a sample swatch.

NATURAL FIBERS

Wool (sheep's wool)

Wool yarns are elastic, and easy and fun to crochet with. They often have a pretty luster, feel soft, and the fabric or project lasts longer. Wool makes warm creations. It is easy to dye wool and it also holds colors well. For those reasons, wool yarns are often available in a large range of colors. Wool which has not been superwash treated can be used to advantage for fulling and felting. There are many special yarns that are suitable to first crochet or knit with and then full or felt.

Lamb's wool is a little warmer than other types of wool and might also be a bit thinner. Merino wool comes from a particular sheep (the Merino) and has very high quality wool.

Mohair comes from Angora goats and makes a very light and warm yarn. Most often mohair is blended with a longer fiber so it will hold together better. The blend might be wool, nylon, or silk.

Alpaca is a very soft wool from the llama family and usually comes from South America. The fibers are long and easy to work with, and the wool is very warm.

Silk

Silk yarns are dense and easily lose their shape, but people who want to crochet small projects and various decorative items often love silk yarns. Silk has a fantastic luster and is comfortable to wear year-round, warm in cold weather and cool in hot weather.

wool yarn

mohair

silk

multi-color silk

Cotton

Cotton is soft both to crochet with and to wear. It is also relatively dense, which means cotton fabrics lose their shape easily when they've been used for a while. On the other hand, a big advantage to cotton is that it can be machine-washed and dried.

Cotton usually has a matte surface but can be processed to be more lustrous. This is called "mercerized cotton." The classic fine crochet yarns, excellent for lace crochet, are usually spun from cotton and can tolerate washing at a high temperature. Cotton is also suitable for crocheted clothing, but you should avoid thick yarns of pure cotton, which will make a thick and clumpy garment.

Linen

Linen is extremely strong and somewhat lustrous. Linen feels hard against the skin and so is often blended with cotton to make it softer and more comfortable to wear. Linen is a very good material to use when it is warm.

Bamboo

Bamboo is a relatively new fiber. It is environmentally friendly because it grows very quickly and doesn't need to be re-seeded or fertilized. Bamboo yarns are very soft and have a natural luster. Like silk, bamboo warms when it is cold and cools when it is warm.

Blends

The development of yarns has grown strong during the past few years. Often different fibers are blended to strengthen a yarn quality. Cotton can be blended with wool, silk with alpaca, bamboo with cotton, etc.

DYED YARNS

The technology of yarn dyeing has also advanced and today many types of multi-color yarns are very popular. In the shops, you'll find a large selection of heathery and striped yarns with different color intervals and more or less soft color shifts. Multi-color yarns have become very popular because they are fun to work with and have surprising color changes.

alpaca

multi-color blend

linen yarn

SYNTHETIC YARNS

Synthetic yarns often have a bad reputation, stemming from the early days of synthetics. The early synthetic fibers were regarded as plastic, and garments made from them pilled quickly. These fibers have developed over time. Today you can find very high quality synthetic yarns. Synthetic fibers are often blended with natural fibers to bring out the best qualities of the material.

Synthetic fibers can be divided into two groups: yarns from the natural world and pure acrylic yarns.

Viscose, acetate, and rayon belong to the natural world. The raw material is cellulose that is transformed from wood chips to yarn through a complex process. These fibers are soft and pliant but dense. Many novelty yarns contain viscose, which can be very smooth.

Acrylic and various polyesters are pure synthetic yarns and even microfibers belong in this category. Acrylic is elastic and easy to work with. It is easy to dye and the dye can be intense and have luster. Acrylic yarns have become popular among those who crochet *amigurumi* (Japanese figures). The yarns are even available as mini-skeins in a wide selection of colors.

cotton and lurex novelty yarn

mini-skeins of acrylic yarns

BALL BANDS

Every ball of yarn is held together with a little paper band around it. This is called the ball band and it contains some very important information. On it, you'll find everything from suggested gauge to washing instructions.

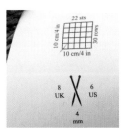

Recommended gauge

Gauge

This symbol stands for the manufacturer's recommendations about what size crochet hook and knitting needles to use. In this case, they suggest working with 22 stitches in 4 in / 10 cm and 30 rows in 4 in / 10 cm.

Washing Instruction Symbols

These are the same as for other textiles.

Washing instructions

Color Number and Dyelot

The shade is the same as the color number and the dyelot indicates the particular dyebath for that skein. Both of the numbers must be the same for all yarn in a project if you want an even result. Different dyelots can have completely different color nuances and can make a big difference in the look of your project. These numbers are stamped somewhere on the ball band. Always check them on every skein when you buy yarn.

Color number and dyelot

Other Materials for Crocheting

What these materials have in common is their relative rigidity. Crocheting with them doesn't go as smoothly as when you use regular yarns. Instead you have to work stitch by stitch— and this takes a little time and, in some cases, strong fingers. However, the result is often worth the effort.

Leather cords

Leather cords are available in several sizes and colors. It can be fun to crochet with leather, but it is often rather stiff. The finer the cord is, the easier it is to crochet with. Leather cords are better for projects like baskets and bags than for garments. Really fine cords work well for jewelry and belts. It can be difficult to find leather cords in local shops, but they are available on the internet.

Plastic ribbon

In the 1960s it was popular to crochet bathmats with plastic ribbon. These strips of plastic have had a renaissance and can be used for much more than just rugs. You can easily make your own ribbon by cutting strips of plastic bags. You can make fantastic patterns and color combinations if you use bags of various colors. Why not crochet large beach bags with plastic?

Fabric strips

Another recycled material offered by stores is strips of recycled cotton knits. This material is easy to crochet with because the strips are elastic. They are rather thick and are suitable for pillows, rugs, bags, and storage baskets.

Of course you can make your own fabric strips. Cut them the same way as for rag rug strips, with the width of the strip proportional to the fabric thickness. Wide strips in a thick fabric are difficult to crochet with. Use fabrics with similar fiber so that you can wash them all together.

Cords

Various types of cords function very well for crochet. Thinner cords are easier to handle than thick ones. Avoid paper cords, which won't tolerate dampness and moisture. In this book, we have used hemp, linen, and cotton cords. Cords are suitable for heavier pieces such as hefty bags, storage boxes, cushions, etc.

Metal

Thin metal thread works well for crochet. The thread must be flexible. Metal is good for crocheted jewelry and baskets.

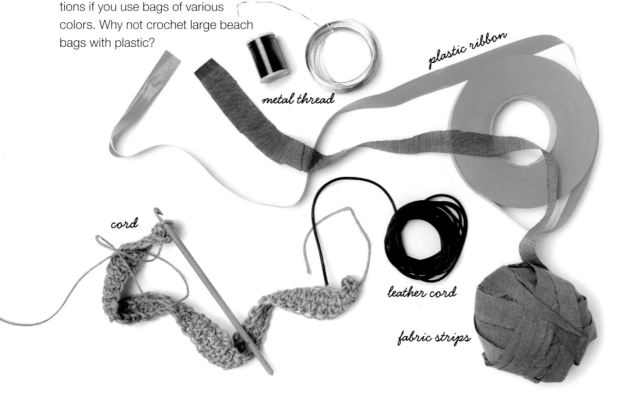

metal thread

plastic ribbon

cord

leather cord

fabric strips

Crochet Hooks

Crochet hooks are made of many kinds of material. The most common are aluminum, steel, plastic, wood, and bamboo.

These days you can also find crochet hooks with different shapes. Some with a thick shaft are ergonomic and squared. Some look like the shaft of a toothbrush in bright colors. Having many crochet hooks to choose from, in various materials and sizes, makes crochet both more fun and easier. In this section, we've included a conversion chart for crochet hooks because many people crochet from international patterns. European sizes are given in millimeters. For the smallest sizes of hook, the size of the hook matches the number—the finer the hook, the lower the size number. In Sweden, these measurements are named after the manufacturer Boye. These very fine hooks are used most often for crocheting lace.

CROCHET HOOKS—SIZE CONVERSIONS

U.S. size	British size	Size in mm
12 steel	5½–6	1 mm
8 steel	3½–4	1.5 mm
-	14	2 mm
B1	13	2.25 mm
-	12	2.5 mm
C/2	-	2.75 mm
-	11	3 mm
D/3	10	3.25 mm
E/4	9	3.5 mm
G/6	8	4 mm
7	7	4.5 mm
H/8	6	5 mm
I/9	5	5.5 mm
J/10	4	6 mm
K/10½	3	6.5 mm
-	2	7 mm
L/11	1	8 mm
M/13	-	9 mm
N/15	-	10 mm
P/Q	-	15 mm

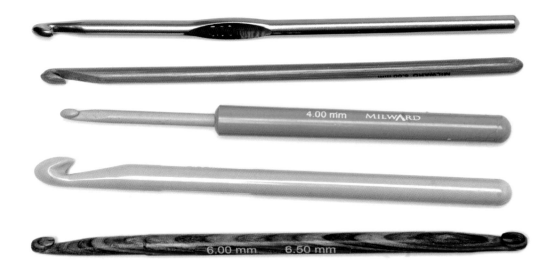

Miscellaneous Equipment

You really don't need too much extra equipment when you crochet: scissors, a measuring tape, and some pins will do, in addition to yarn and crochet hooks. Anyone who still wants to have a little workbox can fill it with a few more practical things.

Below you'll find a number of things that you will need—and some you can do without but might find useful.

Scissors

A small but sharp pair of scissors is all you need. Good plastic scissors are not a bad choice, particularly because they can be taken along on plane trips. If you want to fly with your crochet, you can also buy a "travel sewing kit" at most large airports. They usually contain needles, thread, and buttons, and scissors small enough to get through security.

Measuring tape

Choose a measuring tape at least 1 yard / 1 meter long that will roll or fold up compactly. It is a good idea to have a tape with both inch and metric measurements.

Pins and needles

It is a good idea to have several sizes of needles on hand, some of which should be blunt tapestry needles. Pins, preferably long, are needed to pin together pieces of crocheted fabric; safety pins make good markers.

Yarn swift

A yarn swift is practical if you want to buy yarn in skeins. Otherwise, you have to find a holder (such as two chairs) or a nice person to hold the yarn while you wind it. Old swifts can be found in antique shops and at flea markets, usually cost next to nothing, and are often more attractive than their modern equivalents.

Stitch markers

These small plastic "pins" in bright colors are used to mark stitches and rows. They make it easier to remember where you are in the crochet, and where you need to increase, decrease, or finish.

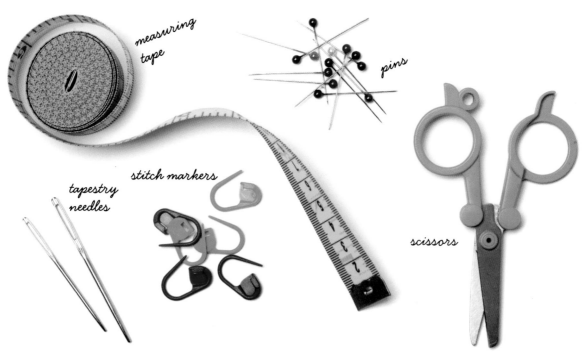

measuring tape

pins

tapestry needles

stitch markers

scissors

Preparing to Crochet

It is such fun to start crocheting right away. Read the first row of the pattern, take out your hook and yarn, and start crocheting. You can solve any problems while you work.

The method above might work very well, but the number of mistakes will be fewer and the final result better if you do a couple of things first to prepare yourself.

What should you do? Here are four simple steps:

1. Read through the entire pattern beforehand to make sure you understand all the abbreviations and symbols. If you don't, turn to page 25 and look over the lists. If what you need isn't there, go back to your yarn store, where you can usually find good help. Many yarn shops will even help you with patterns downloaded from the internet or old patterns if you just ask nicely and, of course, buy your yarn there.

2. Make sure you have all the necessary materials and that all yarns of the same color also have the same dyelot.

3. Crochet a gauge swatch if the size of pattern fit is important. You can save your gauge swatches to make pillows or blankets out of. Gauge swatches are also practical for testing how machine-washable your crochet fabric is. Instead of putting your completed project into the washer, you can wash a swatch and, without any risk, see if the yarn bleeds, shrinks, tears, or behaves in any other way that you wouldn't want to risk on the whole garment.

4. Decide what size to crochet and mark it in the pattern. It is easy to forget this if you set the project aside for a while. Few things are as upsetting as mixing up the sizes while you work on the project.

To crochet a gauge swatch

• Crochet a square piece in the technique given in the pattern for a gauge swatch. Crochet the correct number of stitches and rows to make a piece 4 x 4 in / 10 x 10 cm—but add at least 10 stitches and rows so that you can measure without having to go all the way out to the edges.

• The gauge swatch should actually be about 4¾ x 4¾ in / 12 x 12 cm.

• Lay the swatch out flat and pin it securely to a cushion without stretching it out. Measure out 4 x 4 in / 10 x 10 cm, mark the corners with pins, and then count the number of stitches and rows.

• If the numbers correspond to those given in the pattern, then everything is as it should be and you can just start crocheting. If there are too many stitches, change to a larger size hook; if there are too few stitches, use a smaller hook.

• Crochet a new gauge swatch and measure again.

Developing Your Crochet

You can choose some new ideas and suggestions for your own projects from this pattern gallery. Sometimes we'll suggest how the different patterns can be used and what they are suitable for. We'll also show you how to crochet with several colors and how to change colors.

This chapter also details various ways to embellish and finish your work. A garment worked with simple double crochet can look much more sophisticated with various finishing details such as crocheted buttons, borders, and lace edgings.

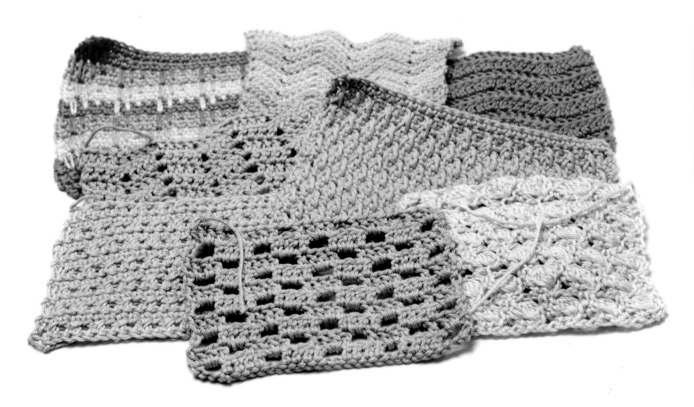

Ribbing & Structure Patterns

These samples show how the basic stitches—slip stitch, single and double crochet—can take on an entirely new look depending on which loops the stitches are worked into.

slip stitches crocheted into back loops

single crochet worked into back loops

single crochet worked into front loops

single crochet worked into back and front loops on alternate rows

Slip stitches worked into back loops

See page 9 for how to work slip stitches. In this case, work all the stitches and rows with each stitch through the back loop of the stitch in the row below.

Slip stitches produce almost no height and so are seldom used for large pieces.

There is a folk tradition of crocheting mittens and stockings with slip stitch. For those patterns, you don't use a regular crochet hook but a tapered, spoonlike tool with a hook at one end. Another name for slip stitch crochet is *påtvirkning* in Swedish and *pjoning* in Norwegian, or tapestry crochet in English. This style of crochet is light and airy, and the fabric is often fulled to make it cold- and water-resistant.

Single crochet worked into back loops

Work regular single crochet stitches (see page 9), but work all the stitches and rows with each stitch through the back loop of the stitch in the row below. Turn every row with ch 1.

This method of crochet can be rather elastic and is sometimes called *rib crochet*. It looks the same on both sides.

Single crochet worked into front loops

Work regular single crochet stitches (see page 9), but work all the stitches and rows with each stitch through the front loop of the stitch in the row below. Turn every row with ch 1. The result will be a flat fabric with relief stripes.

Single crochet worked into back and front loops on alternate rows

Work regular single crochet stitches (see page 9), but alternate rows of stitches worked into back and front loops. Turn every row with ch 1.

Half double crochet worked into back loops

Work half double crochet (see page 10) with the hook inserted into back loop of the stitch below. Turn every row with ch 2.

TIPS & TRICKS

Single crochet worked into back loops makes a very nice ribbed fabric. If you want a ribbed edge for your crochet piece, begin with a strip the width you want for the ribbing. Crochet the strip to desired length. If, for example, you are crocheting a sweater, you can make a strip as long as the back is wide. Next, pick up stitches along one long side of the strip and continue crocheting upwards. Ribbed crochet is also excellent for cuffs and wrist warmers.

If, instead, you are crocheting in the round, and work single crochet into back loops only, you'll get a totally different result. The crochet will be tight and firm with obvious striping. This method of crochet is particularly suitable for mittens and hats made with fine yarn.

half double crochet worked in back loops

Single crochet worked alternately into back and front loops

Multiple of 2 stitches.

+ 1 if you are beginning immediately after the starting chain.

Row 1: Skip 1 ch, work 1 sc in every chain across; turn.

Row 2: Ch 1, 1 sc in the back loop of the 1st st, 1 sc in the front loop of next st, *1 sc into back loop of next st, 1 sc into front loop of next st*; rep from * to * across; turn.

Repeat Row 2.

This method of single crochet corresponds to seed stitch in knitting and produces a firm, structured fabric. It is good for a project that needs to be durable and firm, as, for example, bags, potholders, and baskets. Here's your chance to try out various types of yarn or cord to produce an interesting surface texture.

Half double crochet worked alternately into back and front loops

Multiple of 2 stitches.

+ 1 if you are beginning immediately after the starting chain.

Row 1: Skip 2 ch (= 1 hdc), work 1 hdc in every chain across; turn.

Row 2: Ch 2 (= 1 hdc), skip 1 hdc, *1 hdc in the back loop of the 1st st, 1 hdc in the front loop of next st*; rep from * to * across; turn.

Repeat Row 2.

This fabric looks much like that worked the same way with single crochet, but the half double crochet stitches add height and make the fabric a bit more open. The Chanel jacket on page 99 is worked this way for a "woven" look.

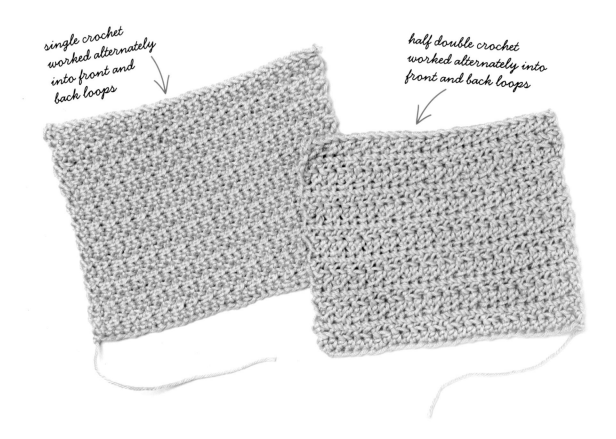

single crochet worked alternately into front and back loops

half double crochet worked alternately into front and back loops

Chanel jacket, crocheted in half double crochet worked alternately into front and back loops (see instructions on page 99).

V-Stitch Double & Single Crochet

Here is a group of patterns formed with various combinations of single and double crochet and chain stitches. Motifs consisting of chain stitches and double crochet are rather airy, quickly grow in length, and are great for clothing. You can combine the stitches endlessly. We'll show you a few examples.

V-stitch Double Crochet

Multiple of 2 sts.

+ 2 ch if you begin immediately after the beginning chain.

Set-up row (RS): 2 dc in the 4th ch from hook, * skip 1 ch, work 2 dc in the next ch; rep from * to the last 2 ch, skip 1 ch, 1 dc in last ch; turn.

Pattern row: Ch 3, *skip 2 dc, work 2 dc between the 2 dc of previous row; rep from * to last 2 sts, skip 1 st, work 1 dc in top of tch; turn.

Repeat Pattern row.

Groups with 2 and 3 V-stitch Double Crochet

Multiple of 6 sts + 2.

+ 2 ch if you begin immediately after the beginning chain.

V-stitch: (1 dc, ch 1, 1 dc) in same stitch.

Row 1 (RS): Begin with 1 V-st in the 5th ch from hook, *skip 2 ch, work 3 dc in next ch, skip 2 ch, 1 V-st in next ch; rep from * across, ending the last repeat by skipping 2 ch, 3 dc in next ch, skip 1 ch, 1 dc in last ch; turn.

Row 2: Ch 3, *skip 2 sts, 3 dc in center st of 3-dc group, then 1 V-st in the center (= into ch loop) of the next V-st; rep from * across, ending with 1 dc in the top of turning ch; turn.

Row 3: Ch 3, *1 V-st in the center of the next V st, 3 dc in the center st of the 3-dc group; rep from * across, ending the last rep with 1 dc in top of tch.

Repeat Rows 2-3.

Groups with Single and Double Crochet

Multiple of 2 sts + 1.

+ 2 ch if you begin immediately after the beginning chain.

Row 1: 1 dc in the 3rd ch, *skip 1 ch, work 1 sc + 1 dc in next ch; rep from * to last 2 ch, skip 1 ch, work 1 sc in last ch; turn.

Row 2: Ch 1 (= 1 sc), 1 dc in 1st st, *skip 1 dc, work 1 sc and 1 dc in next st; rep from * to last 2 sts, skip 1 dc, work 1 sc in the top of tch; turn.

Repeat Row 2.

Single and Double Crochet separated by a chain stitch

Multiple of 3 sts + 2.

+ 1 ch if you begin immediately after the beginning chain.

Row 1 (RS): Skip 2 ch (= 1st sc), *work (1 sc, ch 1, 1 dc) in next ch, skip 2 ch; rep from * across and end last rep with 1 sc in last ch; turn.

Row 2: Ch 1 (= 1 sc), skip 1st sc and dc, *work (1 sc, ch 1, 1 dc) in next ch loop, skip 1 sc and 1 dc; rep from * across, ending last rep with 1 sc, ch 1, 1 dc in last ch, 1 sc in tch; turn.

Repeat Row 2.

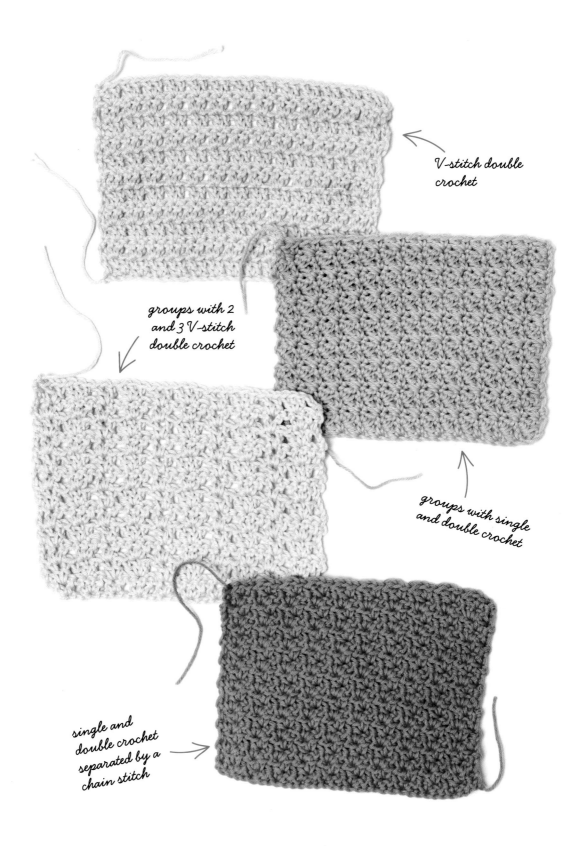

V-stitch double crochet

groups with 2 and 3 V-stitch double crochet

groups with single and double crochet

single and double crochet separated by a chain stitch

Fans & Shells

Fans and shells are fun to crochet. The rows are fast to work and the piece quickly grows in length. Several double crochet stitches are worked into the same stitch in combination with single stitches. Endless combinations of both airy and compact motifs are possible.

fans and V-stitches →

fans ←

large fans and V-stitches →

Fans

Multiple of 6 sts + 1.

+ 1 ch if you begin immediately after the beginning chain.

Row 1 (RS): 1 sc in the 2nd ch from hook, *skip 2 ch, work 5 dc in next ch, skip 2 ch, 1 sc in next ch; rep from * across; turn.

Row 2: Ch 3 (= 1 dc), 2 dc in 1st st, *skip 2 dc, 1 sc in next dc, skip 2 dc, work 5 dc in next sc; rep from * across, ending the last rep with 3 dc in last sc; turn.

Row 3: Ch 1, 1 sc in 1st st, *skip 2 dc, work 5 dc in next sc, skip 2 dc, 1 sc in next dc; rep from * across, ending last rep with 1 sc in top of tch; turn.

Repeat Rows 2 and 3.

Fans and V-stitches

Multiple of 10 sts + 1.

+ 1 ch if you begin immediately after the beginning chain.

V-stitch: (1 hdc, ch 1, 1 hdc) in same st.

Row 1 (RS): 1 sc in 2nd ch, 1 sc in next ch, *skip 3 ch, make a fan with (3 dc, ch 1, 3 dc) in next ch, skip 3 ch, 1 sc in next ch**, ch 1, skip 1 ch, 1 sc in next ch; rep from * across ending last repeat at **, work 1 sc in last ch; turn.

Row 2: Ch 2 (= 1 hdc), 1 hdc in 1st st, *ch 3, 1 sc in chain loop at center of fan, ch 3**, make 1 V-st in next ch; rep from * across, ending last rep at **, work 2 hdc in last sc; turn.

Row 3: Ch 3, 3 dc in 1st st, *1 sc in next ch-3 loop, ch 1, 1 sc in next chain loop**, make a fan in next ch at center of V-st; rep from *across, ending last rep at **, work 4 dc in top of tch; turn.

Row 4: Ch 1, 1 sc in 1st st, *ch 3, 1 V-st in next ch loop, ch 3, 1 sc in ch at center of fan; rep from * across, ending with 1 sc at top of tch; turn.

Row 5: Ch 1, 1 sc in 1st st, *1 sc in next ch loop, 1 fan in center of next V-st, 1 sc in next ch loop **, ch 1; rep from * across, ending last rep at **, 1 sc in last sc; turn.

Repeat Rows 2-5.

Large Fans and V-stitches

Multiple of 8 sts + 1.

+ 1 ch if you begin immediately after the beginning chain.

V-stitch: (1 dc, ch 1, 1 dc) in same st.

Row 1 (RS): 1 sc in 2nd ch, *skip 3 ch, work 9 dc in next ch, skip 3 ch, work 1 sc in next ch; rep from * across; turn.

Row 2: Ch 3 (= 1 dc), 1 dc in 1st st, *ch 5, skip 9-dc group, work 1 V-st in next sc; rep from * across, ending last rep with ch 5, skip last 9-dc group, work 2 dc in last sc; turn.

Row 3: Ch 3 (= 1 dc), 4 dc in 1st st, *1 sc in the 5th st of 9-dc group as on 1st row, *at the same time* catching the ch-5 loop (that is, catching the ch-5 loop as you form the sc so that the loop lies inside the sc)**, 9 dc in the center of the next V-st; rep from * across, ending last rep at **, end with 5 dc in top of tch; turn.

Row 4: Ch 1, 1 sc in 1st st, ch 2, 1 V-st in next sc, *ch 5, skip 9-dc group, work 1 V-st in next sc; rep from * across, ending last rep with ch 2, 1 sc in top of tch; turn.

Row 5: Ch 1, 1 sc in 1st st, *9 dc in center of next V-st**, 1 sc in the 5th st of 9-dc group in V-st below, *at the same time* catching the ch-5 loop; rep from *, ending last rep at **, 1 sc in last sc; turn.

Repeat Rows 2-5.

Finish the pattern on Row 2 or 4, replacing the ch 5 between the V-sts with ch 2, 1 slip st in the 5th st of group, ch 2.

Fans and Waves

Multiple of 6 sts + 1.

+ 2 ch if you begin immediately after the beginning chain.

Row 1 (WS): 2 dc in the 3rd ch, *ch 4, skip 5 ch, work 5 dc in next ch; rep from * across, ending last rep with 3 dc in last ch; turn.

Row 2: Ch 2 (= 1 dc), skip 3 sts, *work (3 dc, ch 3, 3 dc) in next ch**, skip 5 dc; rep from * across, ending last rep at **, skip 2 dc, 1 dc in top of tch; turn.

Row 3: Ch 5 (= 1 tr + 1 ch), *5 dc in next ch loop**, ch 4; rep from * across, ending last rep at **, end row with ch 1, 1 tr in top of turning ch; turn.

Row 4: Ch 5 (= 1 tr + ch 1), 3 dc in 1st ch loop, *skip 5 dc, work (3 dc, ch 3, 3 dc) in next ch loop; rep from * across, ending with skip 5 dc, (3 dc, ch 1, 1 tr) in tch; turn.

Row 5: Ch 3 (= 1 dc), 2 dc in 1st ch loop, *ch 4, 5 dc in next ch loop; rep from * across, ending with ch 4, 3 dc in 4th tch; turn.

Repeat Rows 2-5.

Fans with Picots

Multiple of 12 sts + 1.

+ 1 ch if you begin immediately after the beginning chain.

Picot: (1 sc, ch 3, 1 sl st in 1st chain) to shape picot.

Row 1: 1 sc in the 2nd ch, *ch 5, skip 3 ch, 1 sc in next st; rep from * across; turn.

Row 2: Ch 5 (= 1 dc + ch 2), *1 sc in next ch loop, 8 dc in next ch loop, 1 sc in next ch loop**, ch 5; rep from * across, ending last rep at ** in last ch loop, ch 2, 1 dc in last sc; turn.

Row 3: Ch 1, 1 sc in 1st st, skip 2 ch and 1 sc, *(make a picot in next dc) 7 times, 1 sc in the 8th st**, 1 sc in next ch loop; rep from * across, ending last rep at **; end row with 1 sc in next ch loop; turn.

Row 4: Ch 8, *skip 2 picots, work 1 sc in next picot, ch 5, skip 1 picot, 1 sc in next picot, ch 5, skip 2 picots, 1 dc in next sc**, ch 5; rep from * across, ending last rep at **; turn.

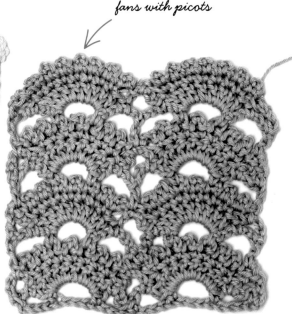

fans with picots

fans and waves

Row 5: Ch 5 (= 1 dc + ch 2), *1 sc in next ch loop, 8 dc in next ch loop, 1 sc in next ch loop**, ch 5; rep from * across, ending last rep at **, ch 2, 1 dc in 3rd st of tch; turn.
Repeat Rows 3-5.

Double Crochet and Half Fans
Multiple of 3 sts + 1.
+ 2 ch if you begin immediately after the beginning chain.
Row 1 (RS): Skip 3 ch (= 1 dc), work 1 dc in each ch across; turn.
Row 2: Ch 1 (= 1 sc), 2 dc in 1st st, *skip 2 dc, 1 sc, work 2 dc in next st; rep from * to last 3 sts; skip 2 sts, 1 sc in top of tch; turn.
Row 3: Ch 3 (= 1 dc), skip 1 st, work 1 dc in each st across, ending with 1 dc in last sc.
Repeat Rows 2-3.

Shells and V-stitches
Multiple of 8 sts + 1.
+ 3 ch if you begin immediately after the beginning chain.
V-stitch: (1 dc, ch 1, 1 dc) in same st.
Row 1 (RS): Skip 3 ch (= 1 dc), 1 dc in next ch, *skip 3 ch, 1 V-st in next ch, skip 3 ch**, 5 dc in next ch; rep from *, ending last rep at **, 2 dc in last ch; turn.
Row 2: Ch 3 (= 1 dc), 1 dc in 1st st, *5 dc in center of V-st (that is, around ch)**, 1 V-st in the 3rd of the following 5 dc; rep from * across, ending last rep at **, 2 dc in top of turning ch; turn.
Row 3: Ch 3 (= 1 dc), 2 dc in 1st st, *1 V-st in the 3rd of the following 5 dc**, 5 dc in center of V-st; rep from * across, ending last rep at **, 3 dc in top of tch; turn.
Repeat Rows 2-3.

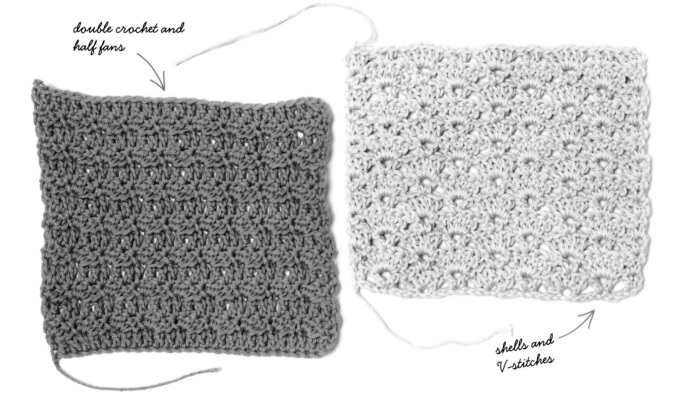

double crochet and half fans

shells and V-stitches

Shells on the Diagonal

Often a group of several double crochet stitches worked into the same stitch is called a "shell."
Multiple of 4 sts + 1.

+ 1 ch if you begin immediately after the beginning chain.

Shell: (1 sc, ch 3, 4 dc) in same st.

Row 1 (RS): 1 shell in the 2nd ch, *skip 3 ch, 1 shell in next ch; rep from * to last 4 ch, skip 3 ch, 1 sc in last ch; turn.

Row 2: Ch 3 (= 1 dc), skip 1st st, *skip 1 dc, work 2 dc tog over the next 2 dc, ch 3, skip 1 dc, 1 sc in top of the ch-3 loop; rep from * across; turn.

Row 3: Ch 1, 1 shell in the 1st st, *skip 3 ch and next st, 1 shell in next sc; rep from * across, ending last with skip 3 ch and next st, work 1 sc in the top of tch; turn.

Repeat Rows 2 and 3.

Baskets

Multiple of 6 sts + 5.

+ 2 ch if you begin immediately after the beginning chain.

V-stitch: (1 dc, ch 1, 1 dc) in same st.

Double V-stitch: (2 dc, ch 1, 2 dc) in same st.

Row 1 (WS): Make 1 V-st in the 5th ch, *skip 2 ch, work 1 V-st in next ch; rep from * to last 2 ch, skip 1 ch, 1 dc in last ch; turn.

Row 2: Ch 3, slip 2 sts, make a double V-st in the center of the V-st below, *ch 1, skip next V-st, make a double V-st in center of next V-st; rep from * across, working the last dc in the double V-st together with the last dc (which was crocheted in the top of the ch-3 turning loop.

Row 3: Ch 3, make 1 V-st in each ch, ending with 1 dc in the top of the ch-3 turning loop.

Row 4: Ch 3, 1 dc in 1st st, *ch 1, skip next V-st, make a double V-st in the center of the next V-st; rep from * across until 1 V-st remains, ch 1, skip V-st, work 2 dc in the top of tch; turn.

Row 5: Work as for Row 3.

Repeat Rows 2-5.

Double Crochet and Chain Stitches on the Diagonal

Multiple of 7 sts.

+ 4 ch if you begin immediately after the beginning chain.

Row 1 (RS): 1 dc in the 5th ch, *ch 2, skip 5 ch, work 4 dc in next ch**, ch 2, 1 dc in next ch; rep from * across, ending last rep at ** in last ch; turn.

Row 2: Ch 4, 1 dc in 1st st, ch 2, skip (3 dc, 2 ch and 1 dc), work 4 dc, ch 2, 1 dc in next ch loop, ch 2, skip (4 dc, 2 ch and 1 dc) **, work 4 dc, ch 2, 1 dc in next ch loop; rep from * across, ending last rep at **, 4 dc in tch; turn.

Repeat Row 2.

This sweet tunic is crocheted with double crochet and chain stitches on the diagonal (see instructions on page 80).

Shells and Chain Stitches

Multiple of 5 sts + 2.

+ 1 ch if you begin immediately after the beginning chain.

Row 1 (WS): 1 sc in 2nd ch, 1 sc in next ch, *ch 3, skip 2 ch, 3 sc; rep from * across, work 2 sc at the end of the last rep; turn.

Row 2: Ch 1, 1 sc in 1st sc, *5 dc in next ch loop, skip 1 sc, work 1 sc in next sc; rep from * across; turn.

Row 3: Ch 3 (= 1 hdc + ch 1), skip first 2 sts, 3 sc, *ch 3, skip 3 sts, 3 sc; rep from * to last 2 sts and end ch 1, 1 hdc in last sc; turn.

Row 4: Ch 3 (= 1 dc), 2 dc in 1st ch loop, skip 1 sc, work 1 sc in next sc, *5 dc in next ch loop, skip 1 sc, 1 sc in next sc; rep from * to last ch loop, 2 dc in ch loop, 1 dc in the 2nd of ch 3; turn.

Row 5: Ch 1, 2 sc, *ch 3, skip 3 sts, work 3 sc; rep from * across, skip 1 sc at end of last rep, 1 sc in top of ch 3, turn.

Repeat Rows 2-5.

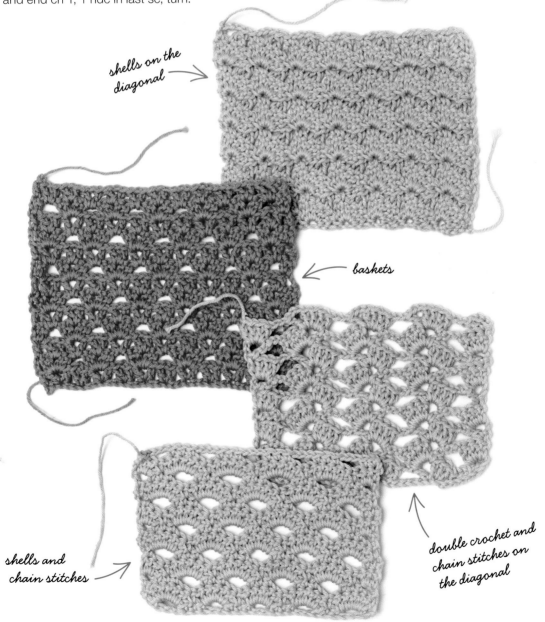

shells on the diagonal

baskets

shells and chain stitches

double crochet and chain stitches on the diagonal

Diagonal Blocks

Multiple of 7 sts + 4.

+ 3 ch if you begin immediately after the beginning chain.

Row 1: Skip 2 ch (= 1 dc), work 2 dc in next ch, *skip 3, ch, 1 sc in next ch, ch 3, 1 dc in each of next 3 ch; rep from * to last 4 ch, skip 3 ch, 1 sc in last ch; turn.

Row 2: Ch 3 (= 1 dc), 2 dc in 1st sc, *skip 3 dc, 1 sc in the 1st st of the ch-3 loop, ch 3, 1 dc in each of the next 2 ch, 1 dc in next sc; rep from *, ending last rep with skip 2 dc, 1 sc in top of turning ch; turn.

Repeat Row 2.

TIPS & TRICKS

If you are crocheting with several colors, change colors between every row so the blocks will be more distinct.

Circles

Multiple of 10 sts + 6.

+ 1 ch if you begin immediately after the beginning chain.

Joining double crochet stitches into cluster: (7, 4, or 3 dc together) = (yarn over hook, insert hook into st, yarnover, bring yarn through, yarnover, bring through 2 loops), continue as set over the number of sts specified in the instructions, yarnover, bring through all the loops on hook.

Row 1 (WS): 1 sc in 2nd ch, 1 sc in next ch, *skip 3 ch, 7 dc in next ch, skip 3 ch, 1 sc in each of the next 3 ch; rep from * to last 4 ch, skip 3 ch, 4 dc in last ch; turn.

Row 2: Ch 1, 5 sc in 1st st, 1 sc in next st, *ch 3, 7 dc tog (= join the next 7 dc into cluster), ch 3, 1 sc in each of the next 3 sts; rep from * to last 4 sts, ch 3, 4 dc tog; turn.

Row 3: Ch 3 (= 1 dc), 3 dc in 1st st, *skip 3 ch, 3 sc, skip 3 ch, 7 dc in center of dc cluster; rep from *, ending last rep with skip 3 ch, 2 sc; turn.

Row 4: Ch 3 (= 1 dc), skip 1st st, 3 dc tog, *ch 3, 3 sc, ch 3, 7 dc tog; rep from * across, ending last rep with ch 3, 1 sc in next st, 1 sc in top of tch; turn.

Row 5: Ch 1, 2 sc, *skip 3 ch, 7 dc in center of 7-dc cluster, skip 3 ch, 3 sc; rep from * across, ending last rep with skip 3 ch, 4 dc in top of tch; turn.

Repeat Rows 2-5.

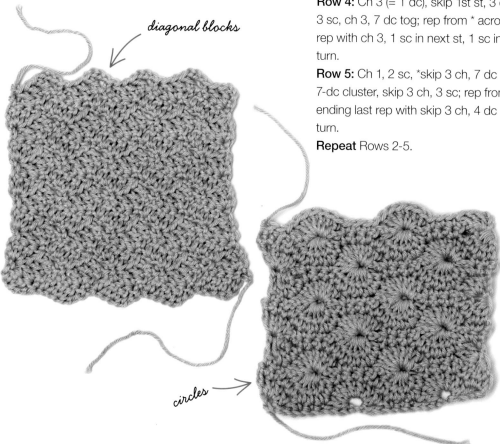

diagonal blocks

circles

Blocks & Lattices

This pattern group is based on the same principle: chain sts and double crochet worked in various combinations to make blocks or lattices. You can easily combine empty and filled blocks to make different pattern motifs.

Net Blocks with chain 1 loop between

Multiple of 2 sts + 6.

Row 1 (RS): Skip 5 ch, *1 dc in next ch, ch 1, skip 1 ch; rep from * to last st, 1 dc in last ch; turn.

Row 2: Ch 4, skip 1st dc, *1 dc in next dc, ch 1; rep from * to last st and end with 1 dc in 3rd of the 4 tch; turn.
Repeat Row 2.

Net Blocks with chain 2 loop between

Multiple of 3 sts + 8.

Row 1 (RS): Skip 7 ch, *1 dc in next ch, ch 2, skip 2 ch; rep from * to last st and end with 1 dc in last ch; turn.

Row 2: Ch 5, skip 1st dc, *1 dc in next dc, ch 2, skip 2 ch; rep from * and end with 1 dc in next ch; turn.

Repeat Row 2.

Filled Blocks

This pattern is formed with double crochet. The filled blocks consist of 1 or 2 dc worked around a chain loop of the empty block. Work the dc forming the block netting as before.

net blocks with ch 1 loop between

net blocks with ch 2 loop between

filled blocks with 1 dc

filled blocks with 2 dc

Simple Lattice

Multiple of 4 sts + 3.

+ 3 ch if you begin immediately after the beginning chain.

Row 1: 1 sc in the 6th ch, *ch 5, skip 3 ch, 1 sc in next st; rep from * across; turn.

Row 2: *Ch 5, 1 sc in next ch-5 loop; rep from * across; turn.

Repeat Row 2.

Picot-edged Lattice

Multiple of 5 sts + 1.

+ 1 ch if you begin immediately after the beginning chain.

Row 1: 1 sc in the 2nd ch, *ch 5, skip 4 ch, 1 sc in next st; rep from * across; turn.

Row 2: *Ch 5, make a picot (1 sc, ch 3, 1 sc) in the 3rd ch of next ch-5 loop; rep from * across, ending last rep with ch 2, 1 dc in last sc; turn.

Row 3: Ch 1, 1 sc in 1st st, *ch 5, make a picot in the 3rd ch of next ch-5 loop; rep from * across, ending last rep with 1 sc in tch; turn.

Repeat Rows 2-3.

Honeycomb is one of several patterns in this dress (see instructions on page 108).

Honeycomb

Multiple of 5 sts + 2.

Row 1 (RS): 1 sc in the 2nd ch and then 1 sc in each ch across; turn.

Row 2: Ch 1, 1 sc in each of the first 2 sc, *ch 5, skip 2 sc, 1 sc in each of next 3 sc; rep from * across, ending last rep with 2 sc; turn.

Row 3: Ch 1, 1 sc in 1st sc, *5 sc in next ch-5 loop, skip 1 sc, 1 sc in next sc; rep from * across; turn.

Row 4: Ch 6 (= 1 tr + ch 2), skip the first 2 sc, 1 sc in each of the next 3 sc, *ch 5, skip 3 sc, 1 sc in each of next 3 sc; rep from * to last 2 sc and end with ch 2, 1 tr in last sc; turn.

Row 5: Ch 1, 1 sc in tr, 2 sc into ch-2 loop, skip 1 sc, 1 sc in next st, *5 sc in next ch-5 loop, skip 1 sc, 1 sc in next sc; rep from * across to last ch loop and end with 2 sc into loop, 1 sc into 4th of the 6 tch; turn.

Row 6: Ch 1, 1 sc in each of the first 2 sc, *ch 5, skip 3 sc, 1 sc in each of next 3 sc; rep from * across, ending last rep with 2 sc; turn.

Repeat Rows 3-6.

Lace Square

Multiple of 5 sts + 2.

+ 2 ch if you begin immediately after the beginning chain.

Row 1 (RS): Skip 3 ch (= 1 dc), 1 dc in next ch, *ch 3, skip 3 ch, 1 sc in each of next 2 ch; rep from * across; turn.

Row 2: Ch 3 (= 1 dc), skip 1st st, *5 dc around ch-3 loop; rep from * across, ending last rep with 1 dc in top of tch; turn.

Row 3: Ch 3 (= 1 dc), skip 1st st, 1 dc in next dc, *ch 3, skip 3 dc, 1 dc in each of next 2 dc; rep from * across; turn.

Repeat Rows 2-3.

Lace Square—Variation

Multiple of 5 sts + 2.

+ 2 ch if you begin immediately after the beginning chain.

Row 1 (RS): Skip 3 ch (= 1 dc), 1 dc in next ch, *ch 3, skip 3 ch, 1 sc in each of next 2 ch; rep from * across; turn.

Row 2: Ch 3 (= 1 dc), skip 1st st, *5 dc in center st of ch loop; rep from * across, ending last rep with 1 dc in top of tch; turn.

Row 3: Ch 3 (= 1 dc), skip 1st st, 1 dc in next dc, *ch 3, skip 3 dc, 1 dc in each of next 2 dc; rep from * across; turn.

Repeat Rows 2 and 3.

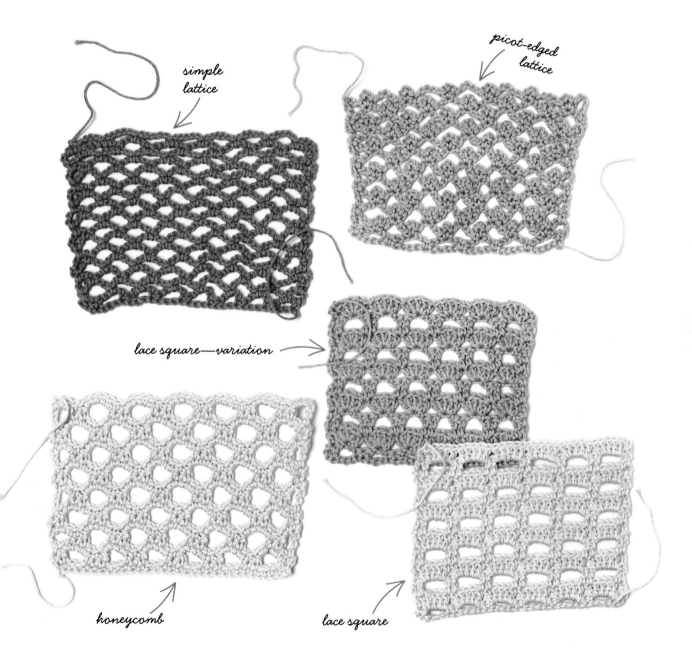

simple lattice

picot-edged lattice

lace square—variation

honeycomb

lace square

Open Blocks

Multiple of 6 sts + 9.

Row 1 (foundation row): Skip 3 ch, 1 dc in each of next 2 ch, *ch 3, skip 3 ch**, 1 dc in each of next 3 ch; rep from * to last st, end last rep at **, 1 dc in last ch; turn.

Row 2: Ch 3, 2 dc in 1st ch loop, *ch 3, 3 dc in next ch loop; rep from * across, ending last rep with ch 3, 1 dc in top of tch; turn.

Repeat Row 2.

Diagonal Blocks with Single Crochet and Chain Loops

Multiple of 8 sts + 2.

Row 1 (WS): Beginning in the 2nd ch, sc across.

Row 2: Ch 1, 3 sc, *ch 5, skip 3 sc, 5 sc; rep from * across, ending last rep with 3 sc; turn.

Row 3: Ch 1, 2 sc, *ch 3, 1 sc into ch loop, ch 3, skip 1 sc, 3 sc; rep from * across, ending last rep with 2 sc; turn.

Row 4: Ch 1, 1 sc in 1st sc, *ch 3, 1 sc in next ch loop, 1 sc in next sc, 1 sc in next ch loop, ch 3, skip 1 sc, 1 sc in next sc; rep from * across; turn.

Row 5: Ch 5 (= 1 dc + ch 2), 1 sc in next ch loop, 3 sc, 1 sc in next ch loop, *ch 5, 1 sc in next ch loop, 3 sc, 1 sc in next ch loop; rep from * to last sc, ch 2, 1 dc in last sc; turn.

Row 6: Ch 1, 1 sc in 1st st, ch 3, skip 1 sc, 3 sc, *ch 3, 1 sc in next ch loop, ch 3, skip 1 sc, 3 sc; rep from * to last ch loop (which has 2 ch), ch 3, 1 sc in the 3rd of the 5 tch; turn.

Row 7: Ch 1, 1 sc in 1st sc, 1 sc in 1st ch loop, ch 3, skip 1 sc, 1 sc in next sc, *ch 3, 1 sc in next ch loop, 1 sc in next sc, 1 sc in next ch loop, ch 3, skip 1 sc, 1 sc in next sc; rep from * to last ch loop, ch 3, 1 sc in last loop, 1 sc in last sc; turn.

Row 8: Ch 1, 2 sc, *1 sc in next ch loop, ch 5, 1 sc in next ch loop, 3 sc; rep from * across, ending last rep with 2 sc; turn.

Repeat Rows 3-8.

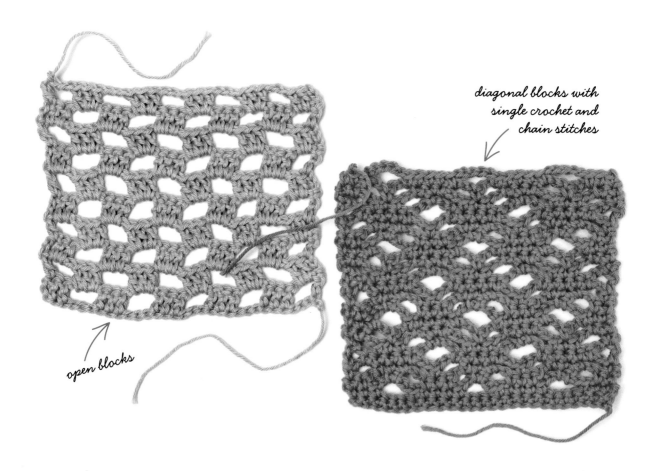

diagonal blocks with single crochet and chain stitches

open blocks

Chevron & Wave Patterns

There are quite a few variations of the basic chevron pattern, most of which are made with double or single crochet stitches. The tips can be made more or less pointy. If you want a shadow effect, work into back loops only. Our swatches were made in only one color but the stripes will really come into their own with changing colors. Chevron stripes are equally nice for pillows as for scarves and shawls. Chevrons also provide a fun way to use up your leftover yarns.

Wave patterns take advantage of the differing heights of crochet stitches. They are easy to crochet but often look more advanced. The waves will look their best in two or more colors.

Simple Chevron

Multiple of 10 sts + 1.
+ 3 ch if you begin immediately after the beginning chain.
Row 1 (RS): Skip 3 ch (= 1 dc), 1 sc in next ch, *1 dc in each of next 3 ch, 3 dc tog worked over the next 3 ch, 1 dc in each of the next 3 ch, 3 dc in next ch; rep from * across, ending last rep with 2 dc in last ch; turn.
Row 2: Ch 3 (= 1 dc), 1 dc into 1st st, *1 dc in each of next 3 sts, 3 dc tog worked over next 3 sts, 1 dc in each of next 3 dc, 3 dc in next st; rep from *, ending last rep with 2 dc in top of tch; turn.
Repeat Row 2.

This pretty shawl is crocheted in a simple chevron pattern (see instructions on page 113).

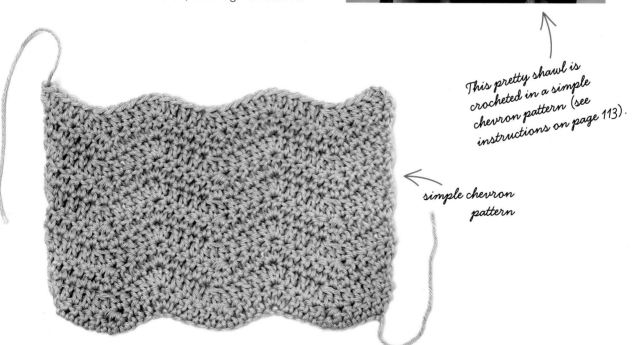

simple chevron pattern

Single Crochet Chevron

Multiple of 11 sts + 1.

+ 1 ch if you begin immediately after the beginning chain.

Change colors after every 4th row.

Row 1 (RS): 2 sc in 2nd ch, *1 sc in each of the next 4 ch, skip 2 ch, 1 sc in each of next 4 ch, 3 sc in next ch; rep from * across, ending last rep with 2 sc in last ch; turn.

Row 2: Ch 1, 2 sc in 1st st, *1 sc in each of next 4 sts, skip 2 sts, 1 sc in each of next 4 sts, 3 sc in next st; rep from * across, ending last rep with 2 sc in last st; turn.

Repeat Row 2.

Chevron worked into back loops only

Multiple of 12 sts.

+ 3 ch if you begin immediately after the beginning chain.

NOTE Work into back loops only.

Row 1 (RS): Skip 3 ch (= 1 dc), 1 dc in next ch, *1 dc in each of next 3 ch, (2 dc tog over next 2 ch) 2 times, 1 dc in each of next 3 ch, (2 dc in next ch) 2 times; rep from * across, ending last rep with 2 dc in last ch; turn.

Row 2: Ch 3 (= 1 dc), 1 dc in 1st st, *1 dc in each of next 3 sts, (2 dc tog over next 2 sts) 2 times, 1 dc in each of next 3 sts, (2 dc in next st) 2 times; rep from * across, ending last rep with 2 dc in top of tch; turn.

Repeat Row 2.

Lofty Double Crochet Chevron

Multiple of 10 sts.

+ 3 ch if you begin immediately after the beginning chain.

Row 1 (RS): Skip 3 ch (= 1 dc), *1 dc in each of next 4 ch, skip 2 ch, 1 dc in each of next 4 ch, ch 2; rep from * to last 6 ch, skip 2 ch, 1 dc in each of next 3 ch, 2 dc in last ch; turn.

Row 2: Ch 3 (= 1 dc), 1 dc in 1st st, 3 dc, *skip 2 sts, 3 dc, (1 dc, ch 2, 1 dc) in next ch loop, 3 dc; rep from * to last 6 sts, skip 2 sts, 3 dc, and then 2 dc in top of tch; turn.

Repeat Row 2.

Soft Waves

Multiple of 8 sts + 4.

+ 1 ch if you begin immediately after the beginning chain.

Stripes: Work 2 rows with color A and then 2 rows with color B.

Row 1 (RS): Skip 2 ch (= 1 sc), 3 sc, *4 dc, 4 sc; rep from * across; turn.

Row 2: Ch 1 (= 1 sc), skip 1st st, 3 sc, *4 dc, 4 sc; rep from * across, working last st in top of tch; turn.

Row 3: Ch 3 (= 1 dc), skip 1st st, 3 dc, *4 sc, 4 dc; rep from* across, working last st in top of tch; turn.

Row 4: Work as for Row 3.

Rows 5 and 6: Work as for Row 2.

Repeat Rows 3-6.

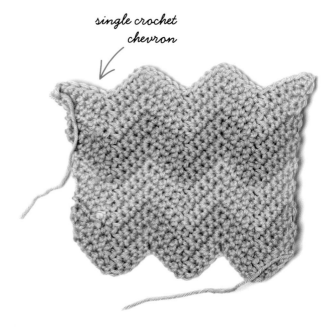

single crochet chevron

Waves with Single, Half Double, Double, and Treble Crochet

Multiple of 14 sts + 1.

+ 1 ch if you begin immediately after the beginning chain.

Group (worked over 14 sts): 1 sc in next st, 2 hdc, 2 dc, 3 tr, 2 dc, 2 hdc, 2 sc.

Reverse Group (worked over 14 sts): 1 tr, 2 dc, 2 hdc, 3 sc, 2 hdc, 2 dc, 2 tr.

Stripes: Throughout, work 2 rows with color A and then 2 rows with color B.

Row 1 (RS): Skip 2 ch (= 1 sc), *work 1 Group over the next 14 ch as described above; rep from * across; turn.

Row 2: Ch 1 (= 1 sc), skip 1st st, sc across, with last sc in top of tch; turn.

Row 3: Ch 4 (= 1 tr), skip 1st st, *work 1 Reverse Group over next 14 sts as described above; rep from * across, ending last rep in tch; turn.

Row 4: Work as for Row 2.

Row 5: Ch 1 (= 1 sc), skip 1st st, *work 1 Group of the next 14 sts; rep from * across, ending last rep in tch; turn.

Row 6: Work as for Row 2.

Repeat Rows 3-6.

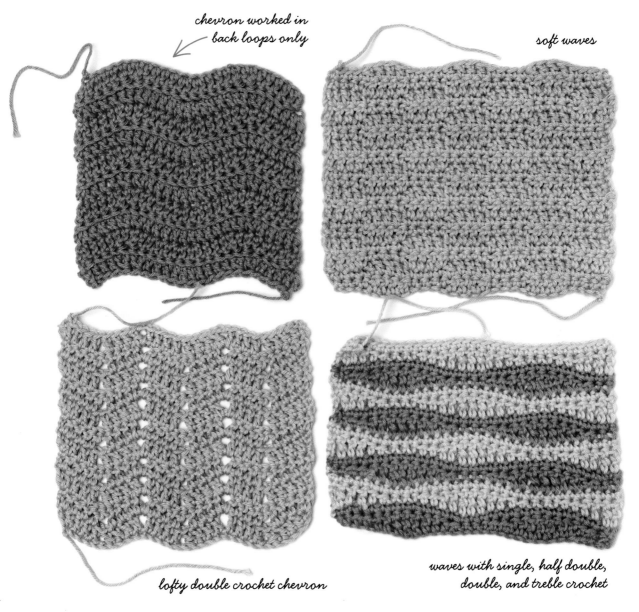

chevron worked in back loops only

soft waves

lofty double crochet chevron

waves with single, half double, double, and treble crochet

Bobbles & Puff Stitches

Bobbles are a group of several stitches worked into the same stitch and then joined into one stitch. They are usually made with double crochet so that the bobble has some volume. If you are designing your own patterns, keep in mind that bobbles require more yarn.

Large Bobbles

Multiple of 4 sts + 3.

+ 1 ch if you begin immediately after the beginning chain.

Bobble (see below): Work 7 dc into the same st and then join them with 1 ch st to pull the loops tightly together (this ch st is not indicated in the pattern). Bobbles usually pop to the wrong side, so don't forget to push them out to the right side of the fabric.

Row 1 (WS): 1 sc in the 2nd ch, *ch 2, skip 1 ch, work 1 bobble, ch 2, skip 1 ch, work 1 sc in next ch; rep from * to last 2 ch, ch 2, skip 1 ch, work 1 hdc in last ch; turn.

Row 2: Ch 1, 1 sc in 1st st, *ch 3, 1 sc in next bobble; rep from * across, ending last rep with ch 1, 1 hdc in last sc; turn.

Row 3: Ch 4, skip hdc and ch, work 1 sc in next sc, *ch 2, 1 bobble in 2nd of the next 3 ch, ch 2, 1 sc in next sc; rep from * across; turn.

Row 4: Ch 3, skip 1st st and 2 ch, work 1 sc in next bobble, *ch 3, 1 sc in next bobble; rep from * across, ending last rep with ch 3, 1 sc in last ch-4 loop; turn.

Row 5: Ch 1, 1 sc in 1st st, *ch 2, 1 bobble in the 2nd of the next 3 ch, ch 2, 1 sc in next sc; rep from * across, ending last rep with ch 2, skip 1 ch, work 1 hdc in center of tch; turn.

Repeat Rows 2-5.

Puff Stitches

Puff stitches are a variation of bobbles. Instead of crocheting stitches to join together, puffs are made by drawing up long loops that are then joined. Puff stitches are loftier than bobbles and form a soft surface texture. They may look difficult but actually are an easy and quick way to enliven a crocheted piece. Puff stitches make a lovely garment detail.

The gauge swatch worked here alternates 1 row of puff stitches with 1 row of single crochet (see instructions at the top of page 59).

BOBBLE

1. Crochet up to the stitch for the bobble. Work 1 dc up to the last step and leave 1 loop on the hook. Into the same st, make a total of 5 dc the same way = 6 loops on hook.

2. Yarn over hook and draw through the 6 loops.

3. Continue crocheting across to the st for the next bobble.

If the bobble pops to the wrong side, simply poke it out to the right side.

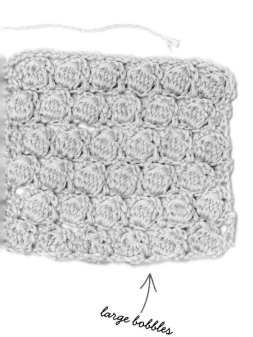

large bobbles

PUFF STITCHES

1. Yarn over hook, insert hook into the stitch where you want to make a puff st, yarn over hook, insert hook into same st, yarnover. Repeat to the desired number of loops on the hook. In this case, we have a total of 7 loops.

2. Yarn over and bring through all the loops on the hook. Make another yarnover and bring through rem loop on hook so the stitch slopes upwards. Continue, following the pattern.

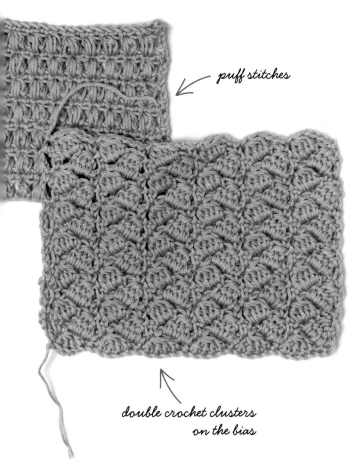

puff stitches

double crochet clusters
on the bias

Double crochet clusters on the bias

Multiple of 5 sts + 1.

+ 1 ch if you begin immediately after the beginning chain.

Row 1 (RS): 1 sc in 2nd ch, *ch 3, 4-dc cluster over next 4 ch (work each dc to last step, leaving loops on hook, yarnover and join the 4 dc), ch 1, 1 sc in next ch; rep from * across; turn.

Row 2: Ch 5, 1 sc in top of dc cluster, *ch 3, 4-dc cluster into next ch loop, ch 1, 1 sc in top of dc cluster; rep from *, ending last rep with ch 3, 4-dc cluster in last ch loop, 1 dc in last sc; turn.

Row 3: Ch 1, skip 1 st, work 1 sc in top of dc cluster, *ch 3, 4-dc cluster in next ch loop, ch 1, 1 sc in top of next dc cluster; rep from * across, ending last rep with 1 sc into last ch loop.

Repeat Rows 2-3.

Crossed Stitches

Crossed stitches are simply stitches that change places with each other. Usually you cross double or treble crochet stitches, which are more flexible. It is an easy way to form various pattern panels. Here are a few crossed stitch variations.

Crossed Double Crochet

Multiple of 2 sts.
 + 2 ch if you begin immediately after the beginning chain.

Crossed Double Crochet: Skip the next st, work 1 dc in next st, go back and work 1 dc in the skipped st.

Row 1: Skip 3 ch (= 1 dc), *work crossed dc over next 2 ch; rep from * across, ending last rep with 1 dc in last ch; turn.

Row 2: Ch 1 (= 1 sc), skip 1 st and then sc across, ending with 1 sc in top of tch; turn.

Row 3: Ch 3 (= 1 dc), skip 1 st, *work crossed dc over the next 2 sts; rep from * across, ending last rep with 1 dc in tch; turn.

Repeat Rows 2 and 3.

You can vary this pattern by using dc or another stitch instead of sc across Row 2.

Waves with Crossed Double Crochet

Multiple of 20 sts + 20 + 1
+ 1 ch if you begin immediately after the beginning chain.

Crossed Double Crochet: Skip the next st, work 1 dc in next st, go back and work 1 dc in the skipped st.

Stripes: Work 2 rows with color A and then 2 rows with color B.

After making foundation chain, work Foundation Rows 1 and 2 and then begin motif with Pattern Row 1.

Foundation Row 1 (RS): Skip 2 ch (= 1 sc), work sc across; turn.

Foundation Row 2: Ch 1 (= 1 sc), skip 1st st, work sc across, ending with 1 sc in tch; turn.

Pattern Row 1: Ch 3 (= 1 dc), skip 1 st, work crossed dc 2 times over the next 4 sts, *10 sc, work crossed dc 5 times over the next 10 sts; rep from * to last 15 sts and end with 10 sc, crossed dc 2 times over next 4 sts, 1 dc in tch; turn.

Pattern Row 2: Work as for Pattern Row 1.

Pattern Rows 3-4: Work as for Foundation Row 2.

Pattern Row 5: Ch 1 (= 1 sc), skip 1 st, 4 sc, *crossed dc 5 times over the next 10 sts, 10 sc; rep from * to last 15 sts and end with crossed dc 5 times over the next 10 sts, 5 sc, with last sc in tch; turn.

Pattern Row 6: Work as for Pattern Row 5.

Pattern Rows 7-8: Work as for Foundation Row 2.

Repeat the 8 Pattern Rows.

crossed double crochet

waves with crossed double crochet

CROSSED DOUBLE CROCHET

1. Make a row of chain stitches. Beg in the 5th chain st, yo twice around the hook. Insert hook into the 5th ch and bring yarn through. Yo and through the first 2 loops on hook = 3 loops now on hook. Yo, skip 1 st, insert hook into next st and bring yarn through.

2. Yo and bring yarn through 2 loops. Yo and bring through 2 loops = 3 loops on hook.

3. Yo and bring through 2 loops. Yo and bring through 2 loops = 1 loop rem on hook.

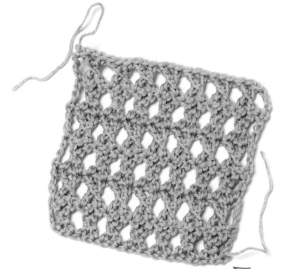

4. Ch 1, yo and insert hook into center of cross where both dc meet and then work 1 dc. Continue with the next crossed dc by making 2 yo around the hook and inserting hook into next st. Begin again at Step 1, and end the row with 1 tr in the top of tch; turn.

Start all following rows with ch 4 and then begin in the 1st st after the 4 ch. Begin the new crossed dc in the 1st st after the previous st so that the crossed dc are stacked one above the other.

crossed double crochet

Relief Stitches

This crochet technique makes, as the name suggests, stitches that stand out from the surface of the crochet fabric. You crochet around the post of the stitch on the previous row rather than through the loops at the top of the stitch. You can either insert the hook in front of or behind the stitch so that the stitch sinks in behind the work or pops out in front.

This technique makes a sturdy and rather dense fabric. You can make relief stitches with single, half double, or double crochet but the most common is double crochet. Relief stitches can be combined in various ways. You can make vertical or horizontal stripes, blocks, or an all-over structural effect. Relief stitches can also produce various shadow effects depending on how you combine them. They are excellent for details on furnishings and as edgings but a complete garment in relief stitches will be heavy and dense.

Special Abbreviations
FPdc: Front post double crochet (the relief stitch is formed on the front of the work—see explanation below).
BPdc: Back post double crochet (the relief stitch is formed on the back of the work—see explanation below).

Front and Back Post Double Crochet Alternating in front of and behind work
Multiple of 2 sts.
+ 2 ch if you begin immediately after the beginning chain.

Row 1: Skip 3 ch (= 1 dc), work 1 dc in each chain across; turn.
Row 2: Ch 3 (= 1 dc), skip the 1st st, *work 1 FPdc around next st, 1 BPdc around next st; rep from * across, ending last rep with 1 dc in the top of tch; turn.
Repeat Row 2.

FRONT AND BACK POST DOUBLE CROCHET

front and back post double crochet alternating in front of and behind work

From the right side:
Begin by working 1 row of regular double crochet; turn with ch 3. Yarn over hook, insert hook from the front and horizontally around the dc of previous row. Catch yarn. Work the rest of the dc as normal. The double crochet will stand upright on the front of the work. On the wrong side, the stitches will form a horizontal line.

From the wrong side:
Work as for the description to the left but insert the hook from the wrong side instead. The stitches will lie behind the work and the stitches will form a horizontal line on the front. The WS will be smooth.

Front and Back Post Relief Stitches with Double and Single Crochet

Multiple of 2 sts + 1.

+ 2 ch if you begin immediately after the beginning chain.

Row 1 (RS): Skip 3 ch (= 1 dc), work 1 dc in each ch across; turn.

Row 2: Ch 1 (= 1 sc), skip 1st st, work 1 sc in each st across with last sc in top of tch; turn.

Row 3: Ch 3 (= 1 dc), skip 1st st, *work 1 FPdc around next st below, 1 regular dc in next st; rep from * across; turn.

Row 4: Work as for Row 2.

Row 5: Ch 3 (= 1 dc), skip 1st st, *1 dc in next st, 1 FPdc around next st below; rep from * to last 2 sts, 1 dc each in last 2 sts; turn.

Repeat Rows 2-5.

Blocks of Front and Back Post Double Crochet

Multiple of 8 sts + 2.

+ 2 ch if you begin immediately after the beginning chain.

Foundation Row (WS): Skip 3 ch (= 1 dc), work 1 dc in each ch across; turn.

Pattern Row 1: Ch 2 (= 1 dc), skip 1st st, *work 1 FPdc around each of next 4 sts, 1 BPdc around each of the next 4 sts; rep from *, ending last rep with 1 dc in top of tch; turn.

Pattern Rows 2-4: Work as for Pattern Row 1.

Pattern Row 5: Ch 2 (= 1 dc), skip 1st st, *work 1 BPdc around each of next 4 sts, 1 FPdc around each of the next 4 sts; rep from *, ending last rep with 1 dc in top of tch; turn.

Pattern Rows 6-8: Work as for Pattern Row 5.

Repeat Pattern Rows 1-8.

front and back post relief stitches with double and single crochet

blocks of front and back post double crochet

Miscellaneous

Dots

Multiple of 7 sts + 1.

+ 3 ch if you begin immediately after the beginning chain.

Work with two colors, A and B. Begin with Color A. Work every other row with Color A and alternate rows with B. Cut yarn after every row.

Picot: Ch 3, 1 sl st into 1st ch.

Picot Wave: 3 dc, 1 picot, ch 1, 1 dc, 1 picot, 2 dc.

Row 1 (with color A): 1 dc in 3rd ch, 1 dc in ch, 1 picot, 2 dc in next ch, *skip 6 ch, work picot wave in next ch; rep from * until 7 ch rem, skip 6 ch, 3 dc, 1 picot, 1 dc in last ch; change to color B, ch 3; turn.

Row 2: Ch 3, 1 dc in 1st st, *ch 3, 1 hdc, ch 2, 1 hdc in center of picot wave; rep from * across, ending last rep with ch 3, 2 hdc in top of tch; turn.

Row 3: Ch 2 (= 1 hdc), *1 picot wave in ch-3 loop; rep from * across, ending last rep with 1 hdc in top of tch; turn.

Row 4: Ch 4 (= 1 dc + ch 1), *1 hdc, ch 2, 1 hdc into ch loop (in center of picot wave), ch 3; rep from * across, ending last rep with 1 dc in top of tch; turn.

Row 5: Ch 3 (= 1 dc), skip 1st st, 1 dc, 1 picot, 2 dc into next ch-3 loop, *1 picot wave in next ch loop; rep from * across, ending last rep with 3 dc, 1 picot, 1 dc in the 3rd of the 4 tch; turn.

Repeat Rows 2-5.

Two-Color Double Crochet Blocks

Multiple of 4 sts + 2.

Work with two colors, A and B. Begin with Color A.

Row 1: 1 sc in the 2nd ch, 1 sc, *ch 1, skip 1 ch, 3 sc; rep from * to last 3 sts, ch 1, skip 1 ch, work 2 sc, ch 3; turn.

Row 2: 1 dc, *ch 1, skip 1 ch, 3 dc, rep from * to last 3 sts, ch 1, skip1 ch, work 2 sc, change to Color B in the last dc, ch 1; turn.

Row 3: 2 sc, 1 tr in the skipped ch of previous row, *1 sc, ch 1, skip 1 st, 1 sc,1 tr in skipped ch of previous row; rep from * to last 2 sts and end with 2 sc, ch 3; turn.

Row 4: 3 dc, *ch 1, skip 1 ch, 3 dc; rep from * to last st, 1 dc, change color in last st, ch 1; turn.

Row 5: 2 sc, ch 1, skip 1 st, *1 sc, 1 tr in skipped ch of previous row, 1 sc, ch 1, skip 1 st; rep from * to last 2 sts and end with 2 sc, ch 3; turn.

Repeat Rows 2-5.

Two-Color Knot Stripes

Work with two colors, A and B. Begin with Color A and an odd number of ch sts.

Row 1: 1 dc in the 4th ch from hook, work dc across. Change to Color B, ch 3; turn.

Row 2: *1 dc, 1 sl st; rep from * across; do not turn.

Row 3: Change to Color A and begin at the same end as for beginning Row 2. Ch 3, work dc across, changing to Color B at end; turn.

Row 4: Ch 1, work in sc across.

Row 5: Work as for Row 3.

Repeat Rows 2-5.

Deep Spike Single Crochet

Multiple of 4 sts + 1.

+ 1 ch if you begin immediately after the beginning chain.

Work with two or more colors.

Row 1: With Color A, begin in the 2nd st and work 1 sc in each st across; end with ch 1; turn.

Rows 2-6: Work in sc across. Change to Color B at end of Row 6.

Row 7: Ch 1 (= 1 sc), insert hook 2 rows down, bring up yarn and work 1 sc (= 1 sc spike). Insert hook 3 rows down, bring up yarn, and work 1 sc. Insert hook 4 rows down, bring up yarn, and work 1 sc. *1 sc in top of next st, 1 sc spike 2 rows down, 1 sc spike 3 rows down, 1 sc spike 4 rows down; rep from * across, ending with ch 1; turn.

Rows 8-10: Work in sc across. Change color at end of Row 10.

Repeat the last 4 rows and change colors after every 4th row. Make sure that the spike stitches stack one over the other; otherwise, it will be difficult to see where the stitches should go and your stitch count may change inadvertently.

Deep Spike Double Crochet

Multiple of 4 sts + 2.

+2 ch if you begin immediately after the beginning chain.

Double Crochet Spikes: Yarn over hook, insert hook into same st as the 1st of the 3 dc, yo, bring yarn through but not too tightly or the stitches will compress; (yo, bring through 2 loops) 2 times.

Row 1: Skip 3 ch (= 1 dc), *1 dc in each of next 3 ch, 1 dc spike, skip next ch; rep from * across, ending last rep with 1 dc in last ch; turn.

Row 2: Ch 3 (= 1 dc), skip 1st st, *1 dc in each of next 3 sts, 1 dc spike, skip next st; rep from * across, ending last rep with 1 dc in top of tch; turn.

Repeat Row 2.

deep spike double crochet groups

dots

two-color knot stripes

two-color double crochet blocks

deep spike single crochet

Woven Crochet

Woven crochet begins with a netting foundation. As the name suggests, this technique produces a woven surface. Begin with a simple double crochet netting or a piece with stripes of open and filled blocks.

Weave or crochet various contrast colors through the empty squares to make blocks and stripes. You can easily create plaid patterns.

Woven crochet can be worked with a variety of materials and for a vast array of products.

TIPS & TRICKS

If you want more thickly filled squares, start with a long chain of chain stitches which you can then thread in as for weaving in stripes.

WOVEN-IN STRIPES

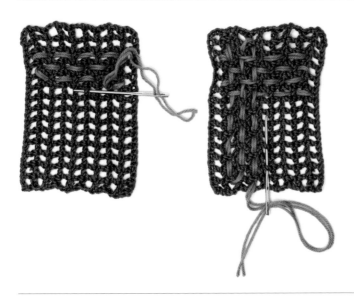

CROCHETED STRIPES

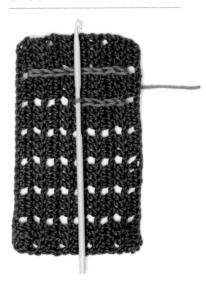

1. Weave the needle alternately under and over the double crochet sts. Use one or more strands.

2. Weave in the needle the same way but perpendicular to the previous row of inlay.

Hold the yarn under the piece and bring up with the hook. Insert hook over next chain st, catch yarn and bring through. Continue to end of row.

Multi-color Crochet

As for knitting, you can crochet with several colors, either in pattern blocks with various colors or in two colors that are carried across the row.

When working multi-color crochet, you work with one color at a time. Twist the colors around each other when they meet, drop the old color, and continue with the new color. Crocheting with several colors this way makes the fabric the same thickness as for a single-color piece.

If, on the other hand, you are working with two colors in blocks, you can catch the unused color with each stitch as you work across or around. Make sure that your tension remains elastic and even throughout. When one color is carried while the other color is crocheted, the piece will be thicker than an item with a single strand of yarn.

INTARSIA

1. Work up to the last step of the stitch with the old color and let yarn hang on the WS. Yo with the new color which had been hanging behind the work.

2. Finish the stitch with the new color. Leave the old color in back of the work until you need to change colors again.

Design Your Own Patterns

It is fun and freeing to create something on your own. Designing a garment isn't impossible but it does require time and patience. Maybe you'll want to design a heavy jacket, a sweater, or a summer top.

Once you've decided what you want to make, you should begin with a sketch of the garment. Consider whether the garment should be close fitting or loose. Do you want a straight silhouette, or one that is tapered or A-line? What type of sleeve would you like: set-in, raglan, or puffy? Should the neckline be round or V-shaped, have a collar or not? Draw the contours of the garment and then take your measurements. Measure around your chest (at the fullest area), the waist, hip bone, and full hip. Measure around the top of your arm, arm length, and length down center back from the nape of your neck to the waist. If you want to simplify matters, measure a favorite sweater that is the same shaping and size as the one you want to crochet.

A simple sketch of the garment is a good way to begin the piece. When you have taken all the necessary measurements and added the desired amount of ease, write down the details on the sketch.

EASE

After all the actual measurements have been taken, you need to add some extra for ease. If you are crocheting a heavy garment, add on at least 4 in / 10 cm for ease. Fine garments need almost no extra ease. Add the ease to the back and front pieces as well as the width of the sleeve. Write down all these measurements for the garment.

NOTE If you have taken your measurements from a finished garment, you do not need to add ease. Draw the garment pieces on pattern paper in full scale as you would for a sewing pattern. This way, you can lay your work in progress on the pattern outline to make sure your piece is the correct size and shape.

YARN AND CROCHET TECHNIQUE

The type of yarn you choose will greatly determine the quality of your garment. A fine yarn crocheted in a sheer pattern makes a light and airy garment. A heavy yarn worked in single crochet will be completely different and make a heavier and less elastic garment. Even the yarn fiber can create a different feeling and look.

It is difficult to calculate precisely how much yarn you'll need. Firmly worked patterns and designs with bobbles take more yarn than open lace work. Just to be safe, always buy a couple of extra skeins.

GAUGE SWATCH

Make several gauge swatches with various patterns and hook sizes. Keep trying until you find the best options. Count and then write down the number of stitches and rows in a 4 x 4 in / 10 x 10 cm square. Also write down the number of stitches and rows in 1 inch for U.S. or 1 cm for metrics.

Get out the paper with all the garment's measurements and begin figuring out how many stitches you'll need.

THE GARMENT

Our calculations are based on a garment with a chest of 37¾ in / 96 cm (with 19 in / 48 cm each for front and back). The length is 23½ in / 60 cm and the sleeve length 18¼ in / 46 cm. The gauge is 20 sts and 12 rows in a 4 x 4 in / 10 x 10 cm square (or 2 sts in ⅜ in / 1 cm and 1.2 rows in ⅜ in / 1 cm). The number of rows per centimeter was calculated the same way. We need to begin with ch 96 (48 x 2), and a turning chain each for the back and front. The length of the sweater is 23½ in / 60 cm or 72 rows. We used graph paper to draw a square 96 blocks

across and 144 blocks long. One block = 1 stitch in width and 2 blocks = 1 row in length. This graph is the schematic for the garment. Because this pattern has high stitches, the number of rows is less than the number of stitches in 4 in / 10 cm. So that the schematic will be proportional and not be misleading, 2 blocks correspond to 1 row in length.

Now you can add in any necessary increases and decreases for the waist or raglan shaping. Draw an even stair step so you can more easily see when you need to decrease or increase. Draw the sleeve the same way. Now you are ready to begin crocheting your garment.

NOTE Don't forget to add extra chain stitches depending on how many turning stitches you need for your pattern stitch.

CROCHET, RIP OUT, AND CHANGE AS YOU WORK

Crochet is much easier than knitting when it comes to trying on and testing. It is easy to rip out a few rows and begin again. Write down all the changes you make so you won't make any mistakes on the next piece.

*Determine the **length** by measuring down the back.*

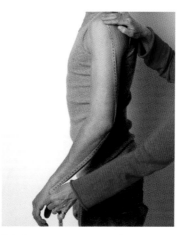

*It is important to get **sleeve length** right.*

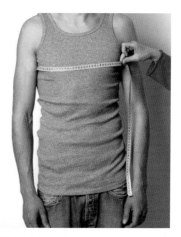

*The **chest circumference** is the same as the bust. This measurement should be taken a bit loosely so that the garment won't be too tight.*

If Something Goes Wrong

Whether you follow a pattern carefully or work freehand, sometimes a project is disappointing. Most often the size isn't correct and is either too small or too big. If you are uncertain about how well a garment will fit, baste the parts together before you sew them. It is much easier to make adjustments before the finishing. Here's how to adjust a few common mistakes:

• **Adjusting the length:** It is easy to shorten or lengthen sleeves: rip out a few rows or crochet some extra. If the sleeve has a sleeve cap or is raglan shaping, you have to rip that section out first, adjust the length, and then crochet a new sleeve cap or raglan. Even the length on the front and back can be adjusted. If the pieces are straight, it is easy to rip out or add a few rows. If the garment is shaped, you can rip down to the beginning of the armhole, adjust the length, and then crochet the armhole again.

• **Adjusting the width:** If the garment is too wide, you can take it in a bit at the side seams. If it is too heavy, you can machine-stitch a tight zigzag inside the extra edge and then cut away the excess. Or, why not add a box pleat at the back neck? Sew down the pleat for a short length and end with a neck edging or collar. If the garment is too narrow, it is easy to add various types of panels and edgings. Crochet edgings along the sides in a different pattern or a contrast color. You can even crochet wider front bands if you don't need to widen the piece more than an inch / a couple of cm.
If you have already sewn the garment together, you have fewer options for fixing it. A garment that is too short can easily be lengthened by adding to the lower edge. If it doesn't work to crochet the same stitches upside down then choose a contrast pattern for a nicer look. If you need to widen the garment, you can undo the side seams and crochet an edging along the sides. Or crochet the sides together with one or two rows of double crochet in between. That way, you can gain important centimeters which would otherwise disappear in the seams. The double crochet stitch is rather tall, so two rows of double crochet at each side can add as much as 1½-2½ in / 4-6 cm of extra width around, depending on the thickness of the yarn.

• **The entire garment is a disappointment:** Try a new finishing detail such as a pretty edging all around or a new collar. Those elements can totally change the look of a piece.

• **The crochet pieces look strange:** It is easy for the rounded edges at the armholes, sleeve caps, and neck to look uneven, particularly when compared to knitting. Many times, this is due to the fact that crocheted stitches are higher than knit stitches and so don't look as even. When the garment is later sewn together, this raggedness can disappear into the seams and the piece will look neater and more even. Depending on the crochet technique, the pieces might look biased and twisted. This usually evens out when the pieces are blocked under damp towels.

Edgings & Embellishments

A good finish is important. Simple edgings or lace borders and crocheted buttons contribute a lot to the final result and can even be used to advantage on knitted garments.

Edgings

Single crochet worked backwards (crab or shrimp stitch): Do not turn the work but, instead, work from left to right in single crochet. These stitches make a slightly pointed edging.

Edgings with chain stitches and picots: Work with a multiple of 3 sts. Insert hook into the 1st st, *ch 3, insert hook in the 2nd ch, 1 sl st, ch 2, skip 2 sts,1 sl st into 3rd st; rep from * across.

Fans: Work with a multiple of 6 + 1 sts. 1 sc in the 1st st, *skip 2 sts, 5 dc in the 3rd st, skip 2 sts, 1 sc in the next st; rep from * across.

Single crochet edging: A row of single crochet is an easy edging. You can either work in the same color as for the rest of the piece or with a contrast color. If the crochet has uneven edges, it will be best if you first crochet a row with the same color as the crochet, which will hide any unevenness, and then change to a different color. At each corner, work 2 or 3 stitches so that the work doesn't pull in. If the piece was crocheted with double or treble crochet, work 2 (for dc) or 3 (for tr) single crochet per stitch/row.

Buttons and Buttonholes

You can crochet over most buttons or even crochet your own simple round buttons. The buttons pictured here were made with single and double crochet. We sewed small glass seed beads to the green button.

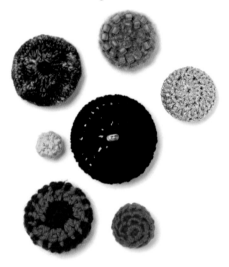

Crochet buttons

1. Begin with a magic ring (see page 13). Crochet around, increasing until the circle is slightly smaller than the button, and then work a couple of rounds without increasing.

2. Place the button in the circle. Cut yarn, leaving an 11¾ in / 30 cm-long tail. Thread yarn onto a tapestry needle and sew through the stitches of the last row. Pull in tightly. Fasten off yarn, leaving enough to sew on button.

3. The finished button.

Buttonholes

Here are three buttonhole variations. Numbers 1 and 2 are worked on the same principle, with one worked across the width and the other length-wise. All buttonhole bands are worked in single crochet for a firm edge. Work to the beginning of the buttonhole; ch 2 or more sts, depending on size of button. Skip the same number of stitches and complete row. On the next row, you can either single crochet around the ch loop or work into the ch sts with the same number of sts as you skipped so that the stitch count remains constant.

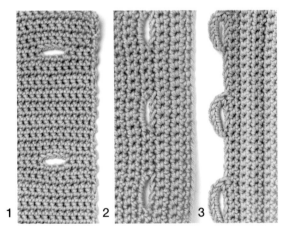

Buttonhole loops (#3) are worked along the edge.
Crochet to the place for the first loop and then continue working to the place where the loop ends. Make the number of chain sts necessary for the size of the button. Turn work and go back to the stitch where the button loop begins, remove hook from chain, insert hook into the stitch on the edge and then work 1 sl st into the ch st so that the ch loop is joined to the edge. Work sc around the loop so it is well covered. Continue along the edge, working the desired number of button loops.

Embellishments

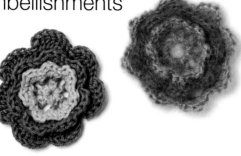

Multi-layer crocheted flower

Ch 6 and join into a ring with 1 sl st.

Rnd 1: Ch 5 (= 1 dc + ch 2), *1 dc around ring, ch 2; rep from * 5 times and end with 1 sl st in the 3rd of the 5 ch = 7 petals.

Rnd 2: (1 sc, 2 dc, 1 sc) into each chain loop around and end with 1 sl st into 1st sc.

Rnd 3: Change color and work dc and ch as follows: Go in behind the first rnd and work 1 dc around the 1st dc, (ch 3, 1 dc around the next dc) 7 times; end with 1 sl st into 1st dc.

Rnd 4: (1 sc, 3 dc, 1 sc into ch loop) 7 times; end with 1 sl st into 1st sc.

Rnd 5: Work as for Rnd 3, but with ch 4 between each dc.

Rnd 6: Work as for Rnd 4, but with (1 sc, ch 1, 3 dc, ch 1, 1 sc) into each ch loop.

Cut yarn and pull end through last st.

Bi-color flower

Ch 8 and join into a ring with 1 sl st. Work around the ring as follows: (Ch 4, 3 tr, ch 4, 1 sc) 5 times = 5 petals.

Change color and begin with 1 sc in 1 sc, *ch 4, 1 sc in each tr, ch 4, 1 sc in sc) 5 times.

Cut yarn and pull end through last st.

Beads

Beads can be worked into all sorts of crochet, but firm crochet stitches such as single and half double crochet hold the beads in place better. String the beads onto the yarn first. Keep in mind that the beads will land on the wrong side.

1. Bring bead up as close as possible to last st worked. Yarn around hook and behind bead. Insert hook into next st and bring yarn through.

2. Yo again and bring yarn through both loops. The bead now sits on the WS of the fabric.

Finishing & Garment Care

Finishing is as important for crochet as for knitting—and you need to take your time for this. It's easy to make a mistake if you are pressed for time. Even a simple potholder is enhanced with even edges and neatly fastened ends. When it comes to clothing, this is even more important. After you've worked hours and hours crocheting, all the styling can be lost if the piece is sewn together sloppily, the buttons aren't directly across from the button-holes, or the neck edge puckers or ruffles.

BLOCKING PREPARATIONS

Take out your tape measure, rustproof pins, hand towels, spray bottle, steam iron, and pressing cloth. Cover a large foam board or table with thin plastic and then fabric or hand towels.

Weave in all the yarn ends, trying to sew them down the sides rather than through the crochet fabric. This method helps keep yarn ends from popping out to the right side.

Spread out the pieces and pin to finished measurements. Spray with water, place hand towels over the pieces, and leave until dry. You can also dampen your crochet work and carefully squeeze the water out or spin in the machine before you block the pieces. Lay a dry hand towel over the pieces and leave them until dry.

Be careful whenever you iron your crochet work. The steam iron can flatten out crochet. Always iron garment seams on the inside. Place a pressing cloth over the crochet work and carefully press with the steam iron. Check the ball band of the yarn for suggestions about how much heat the yarn can tolerate.

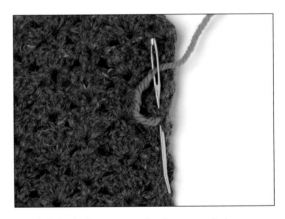

Back Stitch: *Insert needle downwards imme-diately behind the spot where it has just come up and then bring needle out a little further down the seam line. The stitch overlaps on the WS. Back stitch produces a strong and somewhat elastic seam.*

SEAMING

Wait until all the pieces are completely dry. Baste the garment and try it on before seaming. Now pin each seam to make sure that the seams begin and end at the correct places. Sew the

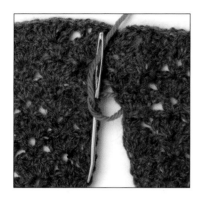

Mattress Stitch: *This stitch is worked with the RS facing. Place the pieces side by side and make a stitch alternately on each side. Tighten the yarn after a few stitches.*

Overhand Stitch *is sewn with RS facing RS.*
1. *Place the pieces edge to edge and sew with small stitches around the outer edge from the WS.*
2. *The seam will be flat when the pieces are turned right side out.*

pieces together with back stitch with WS facing or mattress st with RS facing. Back stitch forms a little ridge on the inside of the fabric. If you sew with the RS facing, there is a finer edge and you can sew stitch by stitch, which is useful when you want the patterns to match at the seams.

Begin at the shoulders and then sew the side and sleeve seams. Sew in the sleeves. Lightly press the seams. Work any crocheted edgings or other embellishments you want. Firmly sew down collars and pockets with overhand st to avoid a small ridge and so that the collar will lie completely flat. Sew the buttons on last.

JOINING GRANNY SQUARES
Weave in all yarn ends. Spread out each block and pin down on a foam or ironing board. Make sure that each corner is pinned at the turn. Spray squares with water and leave until completely dry. You can sew or crochet granny squares together. Use either overhand or back stitch to sew the squares together. If you are joining with overhand stitch, the squares will lie more neatly together if you work through one loop on each square. Back stitch can be worked through both loops.

Crochet squares together with slip st in the back loops so that there is as narrow an edge as possible. Lace crochet blocks are usually crocheted together, sometimes simultaneously with the crochet work.

Begin by crocheting or sewing the squares into a strip the desired length and then join the strips into a rectangle. Press the seams on the wrong side.

Slip Stitch Joins: *Place the squares with RS facing RS. Work slip st through the back loops so that there is as small a ridge as possible.*

CARING FOR CROCHET WORK

Always save the yarn ball band so that you'll have the washing and care instructions for your crochet work. Most yarns are now machine-washable and modern washing machines have excellent wool cycles. You can quickly spin out garments, but tumble drying can easily felt a piece. If you hand wash wool garments, make sure that the washing and rinse water are the same temperature. Big temperature changes can felt the garment. Gently squeeze out as much water as possible but do not twist or wring out water, as that can distort the fabric. Dry and store crochet work flat.

We recommend that you air out your crochet pieces every now and then.

Crochet Patterns

In this chapter, you'll find almost 50 small and large crochet projects at varying levels of difficulty. If you follow the instructions exactly, your project should look just like the one in the pictures. You can also change the patterns for a more personal effect.

Granny Square Blanket

Granny squares are the perfect travel companion. Nothing is easier to take along and work on when the mood takes you. There is always room in your suitcase for a couple small balls of yarn and a crochet hook.

FINISHED MEASUREMENTS
43¼ x 37 in / 110 x 94 cm

MATERIAL
Yarn: (CYCA #3), Rowan HandKnit Cotton yarn (100% cotton; 92 yd/84 m / 50 g) in a variety of colors.

Yarn Amounts: We used about 25 colors of leftover yarns + 1 ball each of Linen #205, Violet #353, Gooseberry #219, and Burnt #353, for the edges.

Hook: U.S. E-4 / 3.5 mm.

GAUGE
One square measures approx. 3¾ x 3¾ in / 9.5 x 9.5 cm.
Adjust hook size to obtain correct gauge if necessary.

GRANNY SQUARE
Ch 6, join into a ring with sl st.
Rnd 1: Ch 3 (= 1st dc), 2 dc around ring, ch 2, (3 dc around ring, ch 2) 3 times, 1 sl st in the 3rd ch. Change color.
NOTE Always begin every round at a corner and end with 1 sl st to the 3rd ch. Cut yarn and pull end through last st. Change to a new color after every round.
Rnd 2: Ch 3, 2 dc, ch 2 and 3 dc in corner loop, ch 1, (3 dc, ch 2 and 3 dc in corner, ch 1) 3 times, ch 1, 3 dc in ch, ch 1.
Rnd 3: Ch 3, 2 dc, ch 2 and 3 dc in corner, [ch 1, 3 dc in ch, ch 1, (3 dc, ch 2 and 3 dc) in corner] 3 times.
Rnd 4: Ch 3, 2 dc, ch 2 and 3 dc in corner, [ch 1, 3 dc in ch, ch 1, 3 dc in ch, ch 1, (3 dc, ch 2 and 3 dc) in corner] 3 times, ch 1, 3 dc in ch, ch 1, 3 dc in ch, ch 1.

BLANKET
Make 108 squares in various color combinations. Weave in all yarn ends. Lightly steam press the squares on the wrong side, covered by a damp pressing cloth. Arrange the squares as you like with 9 squares across and 12 rows. Spread out the colors as evenly as possible. Place the squares with RS facing RS and use back stitch to sew the squares together through back loops. Make sure that you join stitch by stitch so that the squares meet at the corners. Begin by joining each strip of 9 squares and then join the strips. Lightly press the seams.
Edgings: We crocheted edgings in several colors. The long sides are Gooseberry and Linen, and the short ends Violet and Burnt. Begin at a long side and work 4 rows single crochet. Work remaining sides the same way.

TIPS & TRICKS
You can endlessly vary granny squares. The piece will look completely different if you work the last round of each square with the same color. Granny squares are a perfect project for leftover yarns and are best worked with wool yarn. It's also a good idea to choose yarns all of the same fiber and quality so that the blanket will be easier to wash. The thickness of the yarn isn't that important. Heavier yarn will make a larger blanket and vice versa. If you only have yarns in different sizes, fine yarns can be held double.

The blanket can be finished in various ways. A picot edge makes a softer impression than a straight edge. Or use leftover yarns in a variety of colors for a striped edge.

Sleeveless Tunic

A sweet tunic equally good for a quiet walk or wild play. It is cool, pretty, and practical—and just as nice after many washings.

SIZES
1-2 (2-3, 3-4) years.

FINISHED MEASUREMENTS
Length: 15¾ (16½, 18¼) in / 40 (42, 46) cm
Chest: 21¼ (22¾, 25¼) in / 54 (58, 64) cm

MATERIALS
Yarn: (CYCA #1), Schachenmayr Original Egypto Cotton Solids (100% cotton; 197 yd/180 m / 50 g)
Yarn Amounts: 3 (4, 5) balls White #09
Hook: U.S. size D-3 / 3 mm
Notions: 1 button

GAUGE
24 sts and 13 rows in dc pattern = 4 x 4 in / 10 x 10 cm.
Adjust hook size to obtain correct gauge if necessary.

PATTERN
Double Crochet and Chain Stitches on the Diagonal (see page 48)

BACK
Ch 97 (107, 117).
Foundation Row: Beginning in the 3rd ch from hook, work 17 (19, 21) dc, *ch 2, skip 3 ch, 4 dc in next ch, ch 2, 1 dc in next ch, ch 2*, skip 2 ch, work 11 (13, 15) dc**; rep * - ** 2 more times and then * - * once, skip 2 ch; end with 17 (19, 21) dc; turn.
Pattern Row: Ch 3 (= 1 dc), skip 1st st, work 16 (18, 20) dc, *ch 2, (4 dc, ch 2, 1 dc) in the 2nd ch loop, ch 2*, 11 (13, 15) dc**; rep * - ** 2 more times and then * - * once. End row with 17 (19, 21) dc = 95 (103, 111) sts. The ch 2 at each side of the dc panels is not included in stitch count.
Repeat the Pattern Row throughout. Work 8 rows.
On the next row, decrease by working 2 dc tog at the beginning and end of each dc panel = 10 sts decreased across. Repeat the dec row on every 9th row until there are 5 (7, 9) dc between each group with the diagonal dc and 11 (13, 15) dc at each side = 65 (75, 85) sts rem. Continue without further decreasing until dress measures

10¾ (11, 11½) in / 27 (28, 29) cm or desired length to underarm.
Armhole: Sl st across the first 7 (9, 11) (4 dc rem in the outermost dc panels), work across to the last 7 (9, 11) sts; turn = 51 (57, 63) sts rem. Work 3 (4, 5) rows.
Placket opening: Work until 1 st before the center; turn. Now work each side separately, continuing in pattern until armhole measures 4 (4¼, 4¾) in / 10 (11, 12) cm.
Neck: Work across until 11 (13, 15) sts before edge of placket; turn. Work 1 more row over rem sts. Cut yarn and fasten off. Work the other side the same way, skipping the center st and reversing shaping.

FRONT
Work as for back until armhole measures 2 (2½, 2¾) in / 5 (6, 7) cm.
Neck: Leave the center 23 (27, 30) sts unworked. Work each side separately, continuing in pattern until front is same length as back. Cut yarn and fasten off. Work the other side the same way.

FINISHING

Weave in all yarn ends neatly on WS. Block pieces to finished measurements. Cover with a damp towel and leave until completely dry. Join shoulders.

Neckband: Beginning at the back on one side of placket, work the 1st row in sc around the neck and placket, with a multiple of 5 sts + 1. Now make a small scallop edging:

Rnd 1: Ch 3, skip 2 sc, *2 dc, ch 3, 2 dc in next st, skip 4 sc; rep from * around, ending last rep with skip 2 sc, 1 dc in last st.

Rnd 2: *7 dc into ch-3 loop, 1 sc in center of skipped 4 sc; rep from * around.

Make a buttonhole loop on the left side of the back neck. Sew side seams.

Edging around lower edge and armholes: Work as for neckband. Begin at side seam on lower edge and turn after every row.

Lightly steam press seams. Sew on button across from buttonhole loop.

Edged Baby Blanket

Soft colors, soft crochet, a blanket to crawl under and smile contentedly. Anyone who makes this blanket will surely want to crochet another, this time in a larger size for adults.

FINISHED MEASUREMENTS
30 x 34¾ in / 76 x 88 cm

MATERIAL
Yarn: (CYCA #4), Rowan All Seasons Cotton (60% cotton, 40% acrylic; 98 yd/90 m / 50 g)
Yarn Amounts: 7 balls Jersey #191 (beige) and 1 ball each of Iceberg 192 (light blue), Atlas #252 (green), Cosmos #261 (pink), and Denim #249 (dark blue), for the edging
Hook: U.S. sizes H-8 and J-10 / 5 and 6 mm

GAUGE
10 sts and 10 rows in dc pattern with smaller hook = 4 x 4 in / 10 x 10 cm. Adjust hook sizes to obtain correct gauge if necessary.

With Jersey and smaller hook, ch 71 loosely. Beginning in 4th ch from hook, work 1 row dc; turn.

Continue in dc pattern as follows: Begin with ch 3, 1 dc in 2nd st, *1 dc between the next 2 sts, 1 dc in next st; rep from * across, ending last rep with 1 dc in top of beg ch.

Repeat this row to desired length or until you have used 6 skeins of Jersey. You'll need the last skein of Jersey for the striped edging.

NOTE Crochet the edging rather loosely so it doesn't draw in.
Edging: With larger hook, work all around the blanket in sc, with (1 sc, ch 2, 1 sc) in each corner. Work the following rounds the same way, in this color se-quence: Jersey, Iceberg, Atlas, Cosmos, Jersey, Denim, Iceberg, Atlas, Cosmos, Jersey, Denim, Iceberg, and end with 1 round Atlas.

FINISHING
Weave in all ends neatly on WS. Block blanket to finished measurements. Lay a damp towel over the blanket and leave it until completely dry. If desired, lightly steam press the blanket under a damp pressing cloth.

This baby blanket is a great project for anyone just learning how to crochet.

Sweet Baby Dress

Crocheted baby dresses are often cherished as keepsakes for many generations. Not just because they are so durable (they are quickly outgrown) but because they are so pretty.

FINISHED MEASUREMENTS
Length: 10¼ (12¾, 14¼) in / 26 (32, 36) cm
Chest: 19 (20½, 22) in / 48 (52, 56) cm

MATERIALS
Yarn: (CYCA #3), Rowan Milk Cotton DK (70% cotton, 30% milk protein; 124 yd/113 m / 50 g)
Yarn Amounts: 4 (5, 6) balls Bloom #505

Hook: U.S. sizes D-3 and G-6 / 3 and 4 mm

Notions: 1 button

GAUGE
20 sts and 18 rows in pattern with larger hook = 4 x 4 in / 10 x 10 cm. Adjust hook size to obtain correct gauge if necessary.

PATTERN
Row 1 (RS): Ch 1 (does *not* count as 1st sc) and work in sc across.
Row 2: Ch 2 (= 1st hdc) and work in hdc across.
Repeat Rows 1 and 2.

BACK
With larger hook, ch 72 (76, 80). Beginning in 2nd ch from hook, sc across = 71 (75, 79) sc. The entire dress is worked in the pattern above. Work in pattern for 1½ (2, 2½) in / 4 (5, 6) cm. Mark 1 st on each side of the center 23 sts. Begin decreasing on the sc pattern row as follows: 2 sc tog, sc until 1 st before marked st, 2 sc tog, work 23 sc, 2 sc tog (marked st + 1 st after it), work in sc until 2 sts rem and end with 2 sc tog = 4 sts decreased across row—67 (71, 75) sts rem. Decrease the same way on every 4th row 6 more times = 43 (47, 51) sts rem. Continue in pattern without shaping until piece measures 6 (6¾, 8) in / 15 (17, 20) cm.
Armhole and back opening: Sl st over the first 3 sts and then work in pattern to center back, mark center st and turn. Work each side separately. Dec 2-1-1 sts at the side on the following 3 rows for armhole = 14 (16, 18) sts rem. Continue without further shaping until armhole measures 3½ (4¼, 5¼) in / 9 (11, 13) cm.
Neck: Skip 6 sts nearest the opening and dec another 1 st on every row 2 (3, 4) times = 6 (7, 8) sts rem. Work 2 rows in pattern, cut yarn and fasten off. Turn to the other side of neck, skip the marked st and work as for opposite side, reversing shaping.

FRONT
Work as for back, omitting back opening. Begin the neck when armhole measures 3¼ (4, 4¾) in / 8 (10, 12) cm. Skip the center 11 (13, 15) sts = 9 (10, 11) sts on each side of neck. Dec 1 st at neck edge on every row until 6 (7, 9) sts rem. Continue in pattern until front is same length as back at shoulder. Work opposite side of front the same way, reversing shaping.

FINISHING

Seam shoulders and sides.

Neck edging: With smaller hook and beginning at base of back opening, work 1 row sc up sides of opening and around the neck. Work 3 sc at each corner and make a ch-3 button loop on one side of opening. On the next row, work sc around back opening and fan edging around neck as follows: *1 sc, skip 1 st, 5 dc in next st, skip 1 st; rep from *, ending with 5 sc in buttonhole loop. Continue in sc on other side of opening. Cut yarn and fasten off.

Armhole edgings: With smaller hook, work around armhole in sc and then work fan pattern around as for neck.

Lower edge: With smaller hook, begin at one side and make a little picot edging: 1 sc in 1st st, *ch 3, skip 1 st, 1 sc in next st; rep from * around, ending last rep with 1 sl st into 1st sc. Cut yarn and fasten off.

Blocking: Lightly steam press the dress under a damp pressing cloth. Sew on the button opposite button loop.

Children's Hats

Here's a basic hat you can vary in many ways: lace, crossed double crochet, fans, or even add some stripes!

SIZES
1 (2, 3) years

MATERIALS
Yarn: (CYCA #3) Schachenmayr Cotton Time (100% cotton; 96 yd/88 m / 50 g) for white hat and (CYCA #3) Rowan Milk Cotton DK (70% cotton, 30% milk protein; 124 yd/113 m / 50 g) for red hat (shown)
Yarn Amounts: 1 (2, 2) balls White (for white hat) or Red (for red hat)
Hook: U.S. size E-4 / 3.5 mm

SUBSTITUTION
Rowan Handknit Cotton (93 yd/85 m / 50 g), White #263 or Rosso #215

GAUGE
16 sts and 14 rows in hdc = 4 x 4 in / 10 x 10 cm. Adjust hook size to obtain correct gauge if necessary.

WHITE HAT (see photo above)
Ch 5 and join into a ring with 1 sl st.
Work around, placing marker in the 1st st for beginning of rnd.
Note: Begin and end all rnds with 1 sl st into beg ch.
Foundation Rnd: Ch 1, 8 hdc around ring = 8 hdc.
Rnd 1: Work 2 hdc in each st around = 16 hdc.
Rnd 2: (2 hdc in 1st st, 1 hdc in next st) around = 24 hdc.
Rnd 3: (2 hdc in 1st st, 1 hdc in each of next 2 sts) around = 32 hdc.
Continue increasing as set, with 1 more st between increases on each round = 8 inc per round. When there are 80 hdc around, work 2 rnds without increasing. On the next rnd, inc on every 10th st = 88 hdc. Work 5 rnds without increasing and then inc to 96 sts on next rnd. Work 5 (7, 7) rnds without increasing. At this point, you can add or delete rows for a larger or smaller crown.

Brim
Rnd 1: Work around in hdc with 2 hdc in every 8th st.
Rnd 2: Work around in hdc, with 2 hdc in every 9th st.
Rnd 3: Hdc around.
Rnd 4: Work around in hdc, with 2 hdc in every 10th st.
Finish with 1 rnd of crab st (see page 71).

RED HAT (see photo to left)
Work as for above, omitting the brim. Instead, work around, increasing until the hat is large enough. Finish with a picot edging: (1 sc, ch 3, skip 1 st) around.

TIPS & TRICKS
Choose a pattern with a repeat of not more than 1-2 rows. That way, you'll avoid increasing in the pattern area. If you want a wider pattern, work it only within the straight section between the increase lines of the crown.

Blocks Blanket

The first version of this baby blanket was made 30 years ago but it was lost on a train journey in Italy. Now it has been recreated.

FINISHED MEASUREMENTS

42½ x 42½ in / 108 x 108 cm

MATERIALS

Yarn: (CYCA #2), Borgs Vävgarner Tuna (100% wool; 339 yd/310 m / 100 g); any thin yarns can be held double

Yarn Amounts and Colors: We used leftover yarns: 200 g dark green for center of blocks and edging. The rest of the yarns are divided into 2 color groups:
a *light* group with various shades of pink + natural white, light gray, yellow, and beige
a *dark* group with various shades of green + blue, brown, and dark purple.

Hook: U.S. size E-4 / 3. 5mm or a hook size suitable for chosen yarn

GAUGE

An exact gauge isn't necessary. Work blocks with yarn of similar quality and thickness for best results.

BLOCKS

All of the blocks have the same color in the center.

Begin with dark green and ch 13. Beginning in 2nd ch from hook, work 12 sc. Turn each row with ch 1. Work 14 rows in sc and then change colors.

The rest of the block is worked in double crochet. Begin along the last row of the center square: Ch 3 (= 1st dc) and dc across = 12 dc; turn with ch 3 and work 1 row with dc. Cut yarn and shift piece a quarter turn and work 12 + 4 dc along one short side = 16 dc; turn with ch 3 and work back in dc.

Continue the same way—shift by a quarter turn, work 2 rows dc, extending the row with 4 dc over the short side of previous dc row. Arrange the colors so that the first two sides are worked with a color from one color group and the opposite sides with colors of the other group. Work a total of 3 color stripes on each side. The last row has 36 dc.

BLANKET

Crochet the desired number of blocks. Lay the blocks out on the floor and organize them as you like. The blanket should be arranged so that the color groups form diagonal stripes. You could also join the pieces into blocks of 4 squares each so that one color group forms a diagonal block in the center.

FINISHING

Cover the blocks with a damp pressing cloth and carefully steam press the blocks on the WS or spray with water. After the squares are dry, join with sl st into rows and then blocks to form the blanket.

Edging: With dark green, work 2 rounds of 1 sc in each st around, with 3 sc in each corner. Now work sawtooth pattern: Ch 1 (does *not* count as 1 sc), 1 sc in 1st st, *skip 2 sts, 3 dc, ch 3, and 3 dc in next st, skip 2 sts, 1 sc in next st; rep from * to corner st, work 5 dc, ch 3, 5 dc in corner st. Work the same way in each corner. End rnd with 1 sl st to 1st sc.

Lightly steam press edging.

Yoked Child's Sweater

Small children should have lots of sweaters. When crocheted with soft yarn, such as this cardigan, they are both beautiful and easy for the child to put on and take off.

FINISHED MEASUREMENTS
Length: 14¼ in / 36 cm
Chest: 27½ in / 70 cm
Sleeve length: 10¼ in / 26 cm

MATERIALS
Yarn: (CYCA #3), Rowan Wool/Cotton DK (50% Merino wool, 50% cotton; 123 yd/112 m / 50 g) and a contrast color alpaca yarn (approx. 109 yd/100 m / 50 g)
Yarn Amounts: 6 balls Color A (Deepest Olive #907), 1 ball each Color B (Frozen #977), Color C (Larkspur #988), Color D (Rich Red #911), and Color E (Flower #943)
Hook: U.S. size E-4 / 3.5 mm
Notions: 3 buttons

GAUGE
20 sts and 12 rows in dc pattern = 4 x 4 in / 10 x 10 cm.
Adjust hook size to obtain correct gauge if necessary.

This cardigan is worked from the top down, beginning at the yoke.

YOKE
With Color A, ch 63; turn and work 1 row sc.
Row 1: Ch 3, 1 dc in 1st st, *1 dc, 2 dc in next st; rep from * across = 95 sts.
Row 2: Ch 4, *skip 2 sts, 1 sc, ch 3; rep from * to last 3 sts and end with 1 sc in the top of tch = 127 sts.
Row 3: Change to Color B. Ch 3 and 3 dc into 1st ch loop, *4 dc in next ch loop; rep from * across = 128 sts.
Row 4: Change to Color C, ch 1, *5 dc between each 4-dc group; rep from * across and end row with 1 sc in the top of tch = 155 sts.
Row 5: With Color C, sc across.
Row 6: With Color A, dc across.
Row 7: With Color A, sc across.
Row 8: With Color E, ch 4 (= 1 dc + ch 1), skip 1st dc, 1 dc in next dc, ch 1, *3 dc, ch 1; rep from * across, ending with 2 dc in last 2 sts.
Row 9: Change to Color D. Ch 1, 1 sc in 1st st, *ch 2 over the 3 dc, 1 sc around ch loop; rep from * across, ending with 1 sc in last st.
Row 10: Change to Color A. Ch 3, 1 dc around ch loop, ch 1, *3 dc around ch loop, ch 1; rep from * across and end with 2 dc.
Row 11: Change to Color E. Work as for Row 9 but work ch 3 instead of ch 2 over dc.
Row 12: Change to Color D. Work as for Row 10 but work 4 dc around ch loop instead of 3 dc = 208 sts.
Rows 13-15: Change to Color A and work in sc.
Row 16: Change to Color C and work in sc across.
Row 17: With Color C, begin with ch 1 and work in sc across.
Row 18: Change to Color B and ch 3 (= 1st dc). Skip 1st sc, 1 dc in next sc, *ch 2, skip 2 sc, 1 dc in each of next 2 sc; rep from * across.
Row 19: With Color B, ch 1, 1 sc in each of first 2 dc, *1 dc in each of the skipped sc 2 rows below, 1 sc in each of the next 2 dc; rep from * across; turn.
Row 20: With Color B, work across in sc.
Row 21: Change to Color A and work in dc across.
Row 22: With Color A, work in dc across, increasing at even

Your leftover yarns will be perfect for the stripes on this yoke.

intervals across to 216 sts. The yoke is now finished. The rest of the cardigan is worked only with Color A in dc.

Right Front: Begin at right side of yoke and dc over the first 36 sts. Continue in dc, increasing 1 dc at the armhole on every row 4 times = 40 sts. Continue without further shaping until front measures 7 in / 18 cm (measure down from 1st row of front). Cut yarn and fasten off.

Right Sleeve: Work in dc over the next 38 sts of yoke. Continue in dc, increasing 1 dc at each side on every row 4 times = 46 sts. Next, decrease 1 dc at each side on every 4th row until 32 sts rem. Continue in dc until sleeve is 8¼ in / 21 cm long (measure from 1st row of sleeve). Cut yarn and fasten off.

Back: Work over the next 68 sts of yoke. Work in dc and, *at the same time,* increase 1 dc at each side on every row 4 times = 76 sts. Continue without further shaping until back is same length as right front. Cut yarn and fasten off.

Left Sleeve: Work as for right sleeve.

Left Front: Work as for right front.

FINISHING

Weave in all ends neatly on WS. Block pieces to finished measurements. Place a damp towel over sweater and leave until completely dry. Sew the raglan seams and then the side and sleeve seams.

Sleeve Edgings: Work 1 rnd of sc around cuff edge and then 1 round crab stitch (backward sc, see page 71).

Edging: Read this section before beginning the edging. Work 5 rows of sc all around the sweater edges, with 3 sc in each corner on every row so that the edging remains flat. Mark spacing for 3 buttonholes on the right front: one at neck,

one at end of yoke, and one in between. Make the buttonholes on the 3rd row by working ch 2 and skipping 2 sts. On the next row, work 2 sc into each ch loop. Work the 5th row with Color C. Lightly steam press the front edge. Sew on buttons.

TIPS & TRICKS

Our sweater is made in one size only. If you want a smaller or larger sweater, you can crochet fewer or more rows on the yoke so that there will be fewer or more stitches. Make sure you end with a multiple of 5 sts. Each front and sleeve should be ⅕ of the total and the back ⅖. If there are extra sts, divide them over the sleeves and fronts. Crochet the sweater to desired length.

Baby Carriage Coverlet

This coverlet couldn't be cooler. You could just as well call this a baby blanket and change out the vintage baby carriage to a super modern one. This blanket covers it all.

FINISHED MEASUREMENTS
23¾ x 19¾ in / 60 x 50 cm

MATERIALS
Yarn: (CYCA #2), Borgs Vävgarner Tuna (100% wool; 339 yd/310 m / 100 g) and (CYCA #3), Järbo Moa bouclé yarn (82% wool, 12% mohair, 5% polyamide; 164 yd/150 m / 100 g)
Yarn Amounts: 50 g each light gray, medium gray, dark gray, black, and natural white wool yarn + 100 g bouclé in medium gray
Hook: U.S. size H-8 / 5 mm
Fabric: Lining, the same measurements as crochet piece + seam allowances. We used red wool fabric to line our blanket.

GAUGE
18 sts and 11 rows in pattern with yarn held double = 4 x 4 in / 10 x 10 cm.
Adjust hook size to obtain correct gauge if necessary.

Stripe Sequence
* 1 row white, 2 rows dark gray, 1 row white, 4 rows medium gray, 1 row black, 2 rows light gray, 1 row black, 4 rows medium gray; rep from * throughout.
The stripes are worked in Front and Back Post Double Crochet Alternating in front of and behind work (see page 62).

Crocheted Loops
Loops are made on the WS along the edges. Begin at the step where the hook has been inserted in the next st, *wrap yarn twice around your left index finger, insert hook under the yarn where the two wraps cross on the finger, catch yarn, bring yarn though (there should now be 2 loops on the hook), work 1 sc to secure the loop; rep from * across.

COVERLET
NOTE The coverlet is crocheted with yarn held double, except for the loops.
With light gray, ch 94. Beginning in the 4th ch, work across in dc = 91 dc.
Work in front and back post double crochet pattern, beginning with 1 row in light gray.

Continue with pattern and stripe sequence, beginning with Row 1, until blanket measures approx. 22 in / 56 cm, ending with 2 rows light gray.

Loops all around
Change to bouclé yarn and work with a single strand.
Rnd 1: Work all around the blanket in sc with 3 sc at each corner. Turn.
Rnd 2 (WS): Make loops all around, following instructions above.
Repeat Rnds 1 and 2 once more. End with 1 rnd sc. Cut yarn and fasten off.

FINISHING
Pin out blanket to finished measurements. Lay a damp towel over it and leave until completely dry.
If you like, embroider the child's initials and birth date on the lining fabric.
Lay the lining on the blanket with RS facing RS. Sew the pieces together with back stitch, leaving a small opening. Trim the edges and miter the corners. Turn the blanket right side out through the opening and then seam the opening.

Baby Cardigan and Shoes

The short sleeves and the matching little shoes with a narrow crocheted strap make this outfit special. It is easy to crochet and a fun present to give … and to make.

CARDIGAN

SIZES
3-6 (9-12) months

FINISHED MEASUREMENTS
Length: 9½ (11) in / 24 (28) cm
Chest: 19 (20½) in / 48 (52) cm
Sleeve length: 5¼ (6) in / 13 (15) cm

MATERIALS
Yarn: (CYCA #1), Rowan Fine Milk Cotton yarn (70% cotton, 30% milk protein; 164 yd/150 m / 50 g)
Yarn Amounts: 2 (3) balls Scented Satin #088 (MC), 1 skein Jelly Baby #096
Hook: U.S. size B-1 or C-2 and D-3 / 2.5 and 3 mm
Notions: 3 buttons

GAUGE
34 sts and 28 rows with larger hook = 4 x 4 in / 10 x 10 cm. Adjust hook sizes to obtain correct gauge if necessary.

SHOES

SIZE
3-6 months
Shoe length: 3½ in / 9 cm

MATERIALS
Yarn: (CYCA#1), Rowan Fine Milk Cotton yarn (70% cotton, 30% milk protein; 164 yd/150 m / 50 g)
Yarn Amounts: 1 ball Scented Satin #088 (MC), small amount Jelly Baby #096
Hook: U.S. size D-3 / 3 mm
Notions: 2 small buttons

GAUGE
24 sts and 28 rows with 3 mm hook = 4 x 4 in / 10 x 10 cm.
NOTE The gauge for the shoes is different from the gauge for the cardigan because they are worked with different pattern stitches.
Adjust hook size to obtain correct gauge if necessary.

CARDIGAN PATTERN
Foundation Row: Beginning in 2nd ch, work 1 sc, *ch 1, skip 1 ch, 1 sc in next ch; rep from * across.
Pattern Row: Ch 1 (does *not* count as 1 sc), 1 sc in 1st sc, *ch 1, skip 1 sc, work 1 sc in ch; rep from * to last st and end with 1 sc in last st.
Repeat Pattern Row.

CARDIGAN
The cardigan is worked in one piece, beginning at the lower edge of back.
With MC and larger hook, ch 69 (79). Work foundation row and then work in pattern until piece measures 6¾ (7½) in / 17 (19) cm = 68 (78) sts.
Shape armhole at each side as follows: Ch 3, beginning in the 2nd ch, work 1 sc in each of the next 2 rem ch and then work pattern to last st = 2 sts increased. Increase the same way at the beginning of every row 4 (5) times = 76 (78) sts.
Sleeves: Ch 31 (35) at each side. Work Foundation row over the new ch sts and then work in pattern over all the sts = 138 (158) sts.

Continue as set until piece measures 8¾ (10¼) in / 22 (26) cm or desired length.

Neck: Skip the center 26 (30) sts and work each side separately = 56 (64) sts.

Dec 2 sts at neck edge on the next row. Now you are at the shoulder—mark this row as the shoulder seam.

Left Front: Dec 2 sts at neck edge on the next row. Work in pattern for 1¼ (2) in / 3 (5) cm and then inc 2 sts at neck edge on every other row 3 (4) times. Finish with ch 15 (16) at neck edge on the next row = 73 (84) sts. Continue over all the sts until sleeve measures 6¾ (7½) in / 17 (19) cm to cuff. Beginning at front edge, work across to the last 31 (35) sts; turn = 39 (49) sts. Now dec 2 sts on every other row 4 (5) times, skip 31 (35) sts, and continue over rem 34 (39) sts until the front is same length as back from the shoulder.

Right Front: Work as for left front, reversing shaping.

FINISHING

Cover cardigan with a damp cloth and lightly steam press on WS. Seam sides and sleeves.

Edging: Begin at one side, using smaller hook and MC. Work 1 row sc all around the cardigan edges and then change to green. Work another 5 rounds in sc with 3 sc into each corner st and 2 sc tog where the neck curves in so the edging will remain flat. Make 3 small button loops (see page 72) near the neck on the last row. Sew buttons opposite loops.

SHOES

Bottom (sole): With larger hook and MC, ch 17. Beginning in 2nd ch from hook, work 16 sc along one side of foundations chain, ch 1, and then work 16 down other side of foundation chain; turn. Work 16 sc, 3 sc in ch, 16 sc and 3 sc in 1st st = 38 sts. Keep working around, increasing twice more with 3 sc in the center st of each short end = 46 sts. On the next rnd, inc with 3 sc at each side of the center 3 sts = 54 sts.

Next rnd: Inc with 3 sc in the st on each side of the center 5 sts = 62 sts. Work 1 rnd without increasing. Work the rest of the shoe in stripe pattern, beginning with green. Work 2 rnds of each color, changing colors at the short end which will eventually be the heel.

Top of shoe: Work 4 rnds in sc. Place a marker at each side of the center 14 sts on the other short side. Shape the toe over these sts: Work to marker, 2 sc tog, 4 sc, 2 sc tog, 4 sc, 2 sc tog. On the next rnd, work to marker, 2 sc tog, 3 sc, 2 sc tog, 3 sc, 2 sc tog. Following rnd: Work to marker, 2 sc tog, 1 sc, 2 sc tog, 1 sc, 2 sc tog. On the next rnd, work 2 sc tog on each side of the center st. *At the same time,* shape the heel by working 2 sc tog on each side of the center 12 sts.

Work 1 rnd in sc.

Strap: Count out from the heel and work until immediately before the center between toe and heel. Now work back and forth on a strap 3 sc wide; turn every row with ch 1. Make strap approx. 2 in / 5 cm) long and end with ch 6 and 1 sl st in 1st sc (= buttonhole). Sew a button on opposite side of shoe.

Make the other shoe the same way, placing strap on opposite side.

Soft Teddy

Crocheted figures are fun to make and can be used for decorations, pillows, and toys. You won't come across a softer play companion than this one. The teddy works up fast, so why not make two?

FINISHED MEASUREMENTS
Length: 15¾ in / 40 cm

MATERIALS
Yarn: (CYCA #5), Schachenmayr Ecologico (100% wool; 87 yd/80 m / 50 g) and finer contrast color yarn for ears and embroidery

Yarn Amounts: 2 balls MC and small amount CC

Hook: U.S. size E-4 and 7 / 3.5 and 4.5 mm

Notions: Polyester fill, tapestry needle for embroidery

GAUGE
16 sts and 18 rows in sc with larger hook = 4 x 4 in / 10 x 10 cm.
Adjust hook sizes to obtain correct gauge if necessary.

ARMS
With larger hook and MC, ch 3. Work 2 sc in 2nd ch from hook and then 4 sc in the last ch; 2 sc in the same ch as for the first 2 sc. Join into a ring with 1 sl st into 1st sc = 8 sc.

Continue around but turn after every rnd. End all rnds with 1 sl st into 1st sc; turn and work back. Begin all rnds with ch 1 (does *not* count as 1 sc), 1 sc in 1st st. Continue as follows:

Rnd 1: 2 sc in 1st st, 2 sc, 2 sc in each of next 2 sc, 2 sc, 2 sc in last st = 12 sc.

Rnd 2: Work 1 sc in each st. Repeat Rnd 2 until arm is 4¼ in / 11 cm long.

On the next rnd, dec 2 sts = 10 sts.

Cut yarn and bring end through last st. Fill the arm and set aside. Make the other arm the same way and fill.

LEGS
Work as for arms through Rnd 1.
Rnd 2: 2 sc in 1st st, 4 sc, 2 sc each in next 2 sts, 4 sc, 2 sc in last st = 16 sc.

Rnd 3: 2 sc in 1st st, work to last st and end with 2 sc in last st = 18 sts.

Rnd 4: Work as for Rnd 3 = 20 sts.

Rnd 5: Work 1 sc in each st.

Rnds 6-8: Dec 2 sts on each rnd = 14 sts rem.

Repeat Rnd 5 until leg is 5¼ in / 13 cm long.

On the next rnd, inc evenly around to 17 sts; cut yarn and fasten off. Fill the leg and set aside. Make the other leg the same way and fill.

Joining legs: Insert hook into the 16th st of one leg. Ch 1, 1 sc in same st, work 16 sc across, insert hook into 3rd st of the other leg, work 17 sts across = 34 sts total. Begin and end all rounds as before. Now work body.

BODY
Rnd 1: 7 sc, (2 sc each in next 2 sts, 7 sc) 3 times = 40 sc.

Rnd 2: 8 sc, (2 sc each in next 2 sts, 9 sc) 2 times, 2 sc each in next 2 sts, 8 sc = 46 sc.

Rnd 3: 8 sc, 2 sc in next st, 28 sc, 2 sc in next st, 8 sc = 48 sc.

Rnd 4: Work 1 sc in each st.

Rnds 5-8: Work as for Rnd 4.
Rnd 9: 22 sc, (2 sc tog) 2 times, 22 sc = 46 sc.
Rnd 10: Work as for Rnd 4.
Rnd 11: 8 sc, (2 sc tog) 2 times, 20 sc, (2 sc tog) 2 times, 8 sc = 40 sc.
Rnd 12: 18 sc, (2 sc tog) 2 times, 18 sc = 38 sc.
Rnd 13: 8 sc, (2 sc tog) 2 times, 14 sc, (2 sc tog) 2 times, 8 sc = 34 sc.
Rnd 14: Work as for Row 4.
Rnd 15: 7 sc, (2 sc tog) 2 times, 12 sc, (2 sc tog) 2 times, 7 sc = 30 sc.
Rnd 16: Work as for Row 4.
Rnd 17: 6 sc, (2 sc tog) 2 times, 10 sc, (sc 2tog) 2 times, 6 sc = 26 sc.
Rnd 18: 5 sc, (2 sc tog) 2 times, 8 sc, (2 sc tog) 2 times, 5 sc = 22 sc.
Rnd 19: 4 sc, (2 sc tog) 2 times, 6 sc, (2 sc tog) 2 times, 4 sc = 18 sc.

Fill body and then crochet the arms to the body:
Rnd 20: Begin with ch 1, 1 sc, (2 sc tog) 2 times on body, insert hook into 8th st of one arm, work (2 sc tog) 5 times across arm, on body, work (2 sc tog) 2 times, insert hook into the 3rd st of other arm and then work as for first arm; on body work (2 sc tog) 2 times, 2 sc, 1 sl st into 1st st = 20 sc.
Rnd 21: Work as for Rnd 4.
Fill rest of body and continue with head which is worked onto body as follows:

HEAD

Rnd 1: 2 sc in 1st st, 3 sc, (2 sc each in next 2 sts, 3 sc) 2 times, 2 sc each in next 2 sts, 3 sc, 2 sc in last st = 28 sc.
Rnd 2: 2 sc in 1st st, 5 sc, (2 sc each in next 2 sts, 5 sc) 3 times, 2 sc in last st = 36 sc.
Rnd 3: 8 sc, (2 sc each in next 2 sts, 7 sc) 2 times, 2 sc each in next 2 sts, 8 sc = 42 sc.
Rnd 4: Work 1 sc in each st.
Rnds 5-9: Work as for Rnd 4.
Rnd 10: 19 sc (2 sc tog) 2 times, 19 sc—40 sc.
Rnd 11: 18 sc (2 sc tog) 2 times, 18 sc—38 sc.
Rnd 12: 2 sc tog, 5 sc, *(2 sc tog) 2 times, 6 sc; rep from * once more, (2 sc tog) 2 times, 5 sc, 2 sc tog = 30 sc.
Rnd 13: 5 sc, *(2 sc tog) 2 times, 4 sc; rep from * once more, (2 sc tog) 2 times, 5 sc = 24 sc.

Rnd 14: 2 sc tog, *2 sc, (2 sc tog) 2 times; rep from * twice more, 2 sc, 2 sc tog = 16 sc.
Fill head. Work (2 sc tog) around last 2 rnds. Cut yarn, bring end through last st and sew hole together.

EARS

Each ear has an inner and outer part; each piece is the same—crochet 4 pieces.
With smaller hook and CC, ch 5.
Row 1: Skip 2 ch, work 5 sc in next ch, skip 1 ch, work 1 sl st in last ch; turn.
Row 2: Ch 1, (2 sc in each st) 5 times, 1 sc in ch; turn = 12 sts.
Row 3: Ch 1, 2 sc in next sc, 1 sc, 2 sc in next st, 4 sc, (2 sc in next st, 1 sc) 2 times = 16 sts.
Cut yarn and bring tail through last st.
Join two pieces, working 1 sc through both layers along the rounded outer edge. Cut yarn and fasten off.

FINISHING

Weave in all ends neatly on WS. Sew on ears securely. Embroider the eyes and mouth with CC. We used satin stitch for the features.

Chanel Jacket

An elegant jacket you can coordinate with anything from jeans to a fine skirt. The crocheted embellishments and buttons make a big difference.

SIZES
S (M, L)

FINISHED MEASUREMENTS
Length: 22 (22¾, 23¾) in / 56 (58, 60) cm
Chest: 34¾ (37¾, 40¼) in / 88 (96, 102) cm
Sleeve length: 17¾ (18¼, 18½) in / 45 (46, 47) cm

MATERIALS
Yarn: (CYCA #3), Rowan Tweed (100% wool; 129 yd/118 m / 50 g) and (CYCA #1), Rowan Fine Tweed (100% wool; 98 yd/90 m / 25 g)
Yarn Amounts: 11 (12, 13) balls Tweed Muker #587 and 1 ball Fine Tweed Askrigg #365
Hook: U.S. sizes D-3 and E-4 / 3 and 3.5 mm
Notions: 9 button molds, diameter ⅞ in / 22 mm

GAUGE
24 sts and 14 rows in pattern with larger hook = 4 x 4 in / 10 x 10 cm. Adjust hook sizes to obtain correct gauge if necessary.

BACK
With larger hook and Muker, ch 109 (115, 121). Beginning in 3rd ch from hook, work across in hdc = 107 (113, 119) sts. Now work in pattern:

Pattern Row: *1 hdc in front loop, 1 hdc in back loop; rep from * to last st and end with 1 hdc in front loop. Turn every row with ch 2.

Work in pattern until piece measures 4¼ (5¼, 6) in / 11 (13, 15) cm. Now decrease 1 st (by working 2 hdc tog) at each side on every 4th row 3 times = 101 (107, 113) sts rem. Work without shaping for 2¾ (3¼, 3½) in / 7 (8, 9) cm and then increase 1 st (with 2 hdc each in the first and last st) at each side on every 3rd row 3 times = 107 (113, 119) sts. Continue straight up in pattern until piece measures 14¼ (15, 15¾) in / 36 (38, 40) cm or desired length to underarm.

Armholes: Sl st over the 1st 4 sts of row and then work across in pattern to last 4 sts; turn = 99 (105, 111) sts rem. Now dec 2 sts at each side on every row 2 times and then dec 1 st at each side on every row 2 times = 87 (93, 99) sts rem.
Continue in pattern until armhole measures 7 (8, 8¾) in / 18 (20, 22) cm.

Shoulders and neck: Work 20 (21, 22) sts, 2 hdc tog; turn and work back. Shape shoulders: Begin with 2 sl sts, ch 2, 6 (7, 8) hdc, 6 sc, sl st to end of row. Return to the last complete crocheted row and skip the center 43 (45, 47) sts (= neck), begin in next st and finish as for opposite side.

LEFT FRONT
With larger hook and Muker, ch 55 (58, 61). Beginning in 3rd ch from hook, work across in hdc = 53 (56, 59) sts. Now work in pattern and shape left side as for back to armhole. Decrease armhole as for back = 43 (46, 49) sts. Continue in pattern until front is 4 in / 10 cm shorter than back as measured from outer edge of shoulder.

Neck: Beginning at armhole, work 25 sts, 2 hdc tog; turn and leave rem sts unworked.
Shape neck as follows: Ch 1, 2 hdc tog over next 2 sts, 1 sc in next st, finish row in pattern.

The jacket fabric is identical on the right and wrong sides. Tie a thread or place a marker on the RS so you can keep track of where you are in the pattern.

LEFT SLEEVE

Back section: With larger hook and Muker, ch 27. Beginning in 3rd ch from hook, work across in hdc = 25 hdc. Now work in pattern as before. *At the same time,* inc 1 st at left side (with RS facing), on the 4th row and then 1 time on the 3rd row = 27 hdc. Continue without shaping until sleeve is 3½ in / 9 cm long, ending on left side. Cut yarn.

Front section: With larger hook and Muker, ch 31 (33, 35). Work as for back section, reversing shaping (inc at right side). Do not cut yarn.

Crochet the sections together: Work in pattern across the front section to last 4 sts, place back section under the front one with 4 sts overlapping. Make sure that the pattern matches on both sections and work 4 sts through both layers. Complete row, increasing 1 st at the end of the row so that the stitch count is uneven = 55 (57, 59) sts.

Continue in pattern, increasing 1 st at each side on every 4th row until there are a total of 85 (87, 89) sts. Now work without shaping until sleeve is 17¾ (18¼, 18½) in / 45 (46, 47) cm long or desired length.

Work until 2 sts before sl sts of previous row, 2 sc tog; turn with ch 1. On next row, work 2 sc tog over first 2 sts. Continue decreasing 1 st at neck edge until 20 (21, 22) sts rem. Now work without shaping until front is same length as back at shoulder. Shape shoulder as for back.

RIGHT FRONT

Work as for left front, reversing shaping.

Sleeve Cap: Decrease as for armhole shaping on back/front and then decrease 4-2-2 sts at each side on the next 3 rows. Next, dec 1 st at each side on every other row until 53 (55, 57) sts rem. Now dec 1 st at each side on every row until 43 (45, 47) hdc rem and then dec 2 sts at each side once = 39 (41, 43) sts rem. On the next 3 rows, eliminate 4 sts at each side and end by leaving the rem 15 (17, 19) sts unworked.

RIGHT SLEEVE

Work as for left sleeve, reversing shaping.

FINISHING

Block pieces to finished measurements and lay a damp towel over them. Leave until completely dry.

Seam the sides, leaving 4 in / 10 cm open at lower edge for slit. Seam shoulders.

Front bands and neckband: With smaller hook and Muker, work 1 row of sc around front edges and neck.

Continue in sc but work into back loops only on RS and front loops on WS, working 3 sc into the same st at each corner and 2 sc tog where neck is rounded to keep bands flat. Turn each row with ch 1.

Work 4 rows as above and then work buttonholes on next row: Beginning at neck, ch 4, skip 4 sts, 13 (14, 15) sc through back loops, *ch 4, skip 4 sts, work 13 (14, 15) sc through back loops;

The decorative contrast color makes a big difference in the look of this jacket.

rep from * another 3 times (= 5 buttonholes), complete row. Work 4 more rows as before and then end with 1 row crab st (see page 71).

Seam sleeves. Work 1 row sc and then 1 row crab st around slit and lower edge of cuff.

Large pocket flap (make 2): With larger hook and Muker, ch 27. Beginning in 2nd ch from hook, work in hdc across. Work 2 rows in pattern and then dec 1 st at each side on the next row. Work 1 row in crab st along short sides and rounded edge.

Small pocket flap (make 2): Work as for large flap but begin with ch 23 and work only 1 pattern row.

Buttons: Fill the button mold with straight stitches in MC. End with decorative stitches in navy blue. See picture on page 99.

Edging around jacket and sleeves: Work a picot edging around the jacket as follows: With Askrigg and smaller hook, insert hook into edge and work 1 st per row inside the outer edge. Work *ch 3, 1 sl st into 1st ch (= picot), ch 1, yarn over hook, insert hook 2 sts before the previous insertion; rep from * around edge. Cut yarn and fasten off. Work edging the same way around sleeve cuffs and pocket flaps.

Sewing on pockets and buttons: Securely sew the large pocket flaps on fronts, 1¼ in / 3 cm from seamline and 6 in / 15 cm from lower edge. Sew on small flaps at chest level, centered over large flaps below. Sew 2 buttons to sleeves, overlap the slits and sew through both layers. Sew 5 buttons on front, across from buttonholes.

Vest

This check patterned vest has a single color back. Of course, you can also make the entire vest in one color, or with the pattern on both front and back.

VEST

SIZES
S (M, L)

FINISHED MEASUREMENTS
Length: 23¼ (24, 25¼) in / 59 (61, 64) cm
Chest: 40½ (43, 45¼) in / 103 (109, 115) cm

MATERIALS
Yarn: (CYCA #3), Rowan Felted Tweed DK (50% Merino wool, 25% rayon, 25% alpaca; 191 yd/175 m / 50 g)
Yarn Amounts: 4 (4, 5) balls Seasalter #178 (Color A) and 2 balls Scree #165 (Color B)
Hook: U.S. size E-4 / 3.5 mm

GAUGE
19 sts and 16 rows in hdc pattern = 4 x 4 in / 10 x 10 cm.
Adjust hook size to obtain correct gauge if necessary.

BOWTIE

FINISHED MEASUREMENTS
Width: 6 in / 15 cm
Length: 2¼ in / 5.5 cm

MATERIALS
Yarn: (CYCA #2), sport-weight fine mohair yarn (approx. 125 yd/115 m / 25 g) and a small amount of contrast color for embroidery
Yarn Amounts: 25 g MC
Notions: elastic with buttonhole, ⅝ in / 1.5 cm wide; 1 button
Hook: U.S. size E-4 / 3.5 mm

GAUGE
14 sts and 14 rows in sc with yarn held double = 2 x 2 in / 5 x 5 cm
Adjust hook size to obtain correct gauge if necessary.

PATTERN
Two-Color Double Crochet Blocks (see page 64). Begin on Row 2 and substitute hdc for dc and dc instead for tr; turn with ch 2.

BACK
With color A, ch 19 for ribbing. Begin in the 2nd ch from hook and work in sc across = 18 sc. Turn every row with ch 1 and work across in sc into back loops until there are 50 (53, 56) ridges = 100 (106, 112) sc rows.
Continue along one long side and work 1 sc in every row = 100 (106, 112) sts. Now work in hdc until piece, including ribbing, measures 14¼ (15, 15) in / 36 (38, 38) cm or desired length.
Armholes: Sl st over the 1st 10 sts and then work in hdc to last 10 sts; turn = 80 (86, 92) hdc. Now dec 2 sts at each side on every row 2 times and then 1 st at each side on each row 3 times = 66 (72, 78) hdc. Continue without further shaping until armhole measures 9 (9, 10¼) in / 23 (23, 26) cm.
Shoulders and Neck: Work 20 (21, 22) hdc, 2 hdc tog; turn and work back. *At the same time*, shape shoulder as follows: Begin with ch 1, work 7 (8, 9) hdc, work 7 (8, 9) sc

and finish row with sl st. Leave the center 26 (30, 34) sts un-worked for neck. Work the other side as for first, reversing shaping.

FRONT

Work the ribbing as for back. Sc along one long side, *at the same time*, increasing evenly across to 112 (121, 130) sc.

NOTE There are more stitches on the front than the back because the pattern draws in somewhat.

Work in pattern (see above) with Colors A and B until front is same length as back to underarm.

Armholes: Sl st over the 1st 12 sts, work in pattern to last 12 sts; turn = 88 (97, 106) sts. Now dec 2 sts at each side on every row 2 times and then 1 st at each side on each row 2 times = 76 (85, 94) sts.

On Size M, dec 1 more st at the side = 84 sts. Now shape V-neck as follows:

Work 38 (42, 47) sts; turn. Work each side separately. Continuing in pattern, dec 1 st at neck edge on every row 4 times and then on every other row until 23 (24, 25) sts rem.

Continue without shaping until front is same length as back to shoulder.

Shape shoulder: Beginning at armhole edge, work 7 sl sts, 8 (8, 9) sc, and then hdc to end of row. Work the other side the same way, reversing shaping.

FINISHING

Weave in all ends neatly on WS. Block pieces to finished measurements. Lay a damp towel over vest and leave until completely dry.

Join shoulders.

Neckband: With Color A, ch 7. Beginning in 2nd ch from hook, sc across. Continue ribbing as for lower edge of vest until strip fits around neck when slightly stretched. Overlap ends at base of V-neck. With WS facing, sew down with overhand stitch.

Armhole bands: Work as for neckband until strip fits around armhole when slightly stretched. With WS facing, sew down with overhand stitch.

Final steps: Seam sides. Lightly steam press all seams.

BOWTIE

With yarn held double, ch 16. Beginning in 2nd ch from hook, work sc across = 15 sc. Make a strip of sc 11¾ in / 30 cm long.

Cut yarn and pull end through last st.

Band: With yarn held double, ch 8. Beginning in 2nd ch from hook, work sc across = 7 sc. Make a strip of sc 3¼ in / 8 cm long. Cut yarn and pull end through last st.

FINISHING

Weave in all ends neatly on WS. Embellish the tie as you like. The bowtie in the photos was embroidered with cross stitch in a contrast color yarn.

Lightly steam press the strips on the wrong side under a damp pressing cloth.

Seam the short ends of the larger strip. The seam will be at the center of the tie. Sew the short band around the bowtie, easing in the tie at the same time. Thread the elastic through the band. Sew a button securely to one end and button it through the hole in the elastic.

Sheer Top

A light wool yarn edging makes this straight top much softer. It will be just as pretty for everyday use as for a party, depending on what you wear with it.

SIZES
S (M, L)

FINISHED MEASUREMENTS
Length: 19 (20½, 22) in / 48 (52, 56) cm
Chest: 31½ (35½, 39½) in / 80 (90, 100) cm

MATERIALS
Yarn: (CYCA #1), Rowan Siena 4 ply (100% cotton; 153 yd/140 m / 50 g) and (CYCA#0) Rowan Kid Silk Haze mohair/silk blend yarn (70% mohair, 30% silk; 229 yd/210 m / 25 g)
Yarn Amounts: 5 (6, 7) skeins Siena White #651, and 1 skein Kid Silk Haze Grace #580 for edgings and neck ruffle
Hook: U.S. size D-3 / 3 mm

GAUGE
20 sts and 13 rows in pattern = 4 x 4 in / 10 x 10 cm.
Adjust hook size to obtain correct gauge if necessary.

BACK and FRONT (both worked alike)
With White, ch 84 (94, 104).
Foundation Row: 1 dc in 4th ch from hook, skip 1 ch, *1 V-st (= 1 dc, ch 1, 1 dc) in next st, skip 1 ch; rep from * across = 39 (44, 49) V-sts.
Continue in pattern as follows: Ch 3 (tch), 1 dc in 1st ch loop, *1 V-st in each V-st across. This row is repeated throughout. Work 7 rows in pattern and then dec 1 st at each side on every row 3 times; continue without further shaping until piece is 5¼ in / 13 cm long. Inc 1 st at each side on every row 3 times = 80 (90, 100) sts. Continue straight up until piece measures 11¾ (12¾, 13½) in / 30 (32, 34) cm.
Armholes: Eliminate 3-2-1-1-1 sts at each side over the next 5 rows. Eliminate sts by working sl st over the 1st st(s) and turning when at the same number of sts before the end of the row. The easiest way to dec 1 st at each side is to work 2 sts tog. Now dec 1 st at each side on every other row 2 times = 60 (70, 80) sts rem.
Neck: When armhole is 3¾ (4, 4¼) in / 9 (10, 11) cm long, leave 36 sts at the center for the neck and work each side separately.

At armhole side, dec 1 st on every other row 2 times and at neck edge dec 1 st on every other row 4 times = 6 (11, 16) sts rem. Continue in pattern until armhole measures 7 (8, 8¾) in / 8 (20, 22) cm. Work the other side the same way, reversing shaping.

FINISHING
Block pieces to finished measurements. Lay a damp towel over pieces and leave until completely dry.
Seam sides, leaving the lower 2¾ in / 7 cm open for slit. Join shoulders.
Edgings for lower edge and armholes: With Grace and beginning at side seam slit, work around lower edge with sc, with 3 sc in each corner and 2 sc tog at top of slit so that the edging remains flat. Work another 2 rounds of sc the same way.
Ruffle around neck: With Grace, work around neck with 1 rnd sc. Now work ruffle as follows: Begin with ch 3 and then work 3 dc in each st around and then work 1 rnd with 1 dc in each st.
Final Steps: Cut yarn and fasten off. Lightly steam press seams.

Open Cardigan

Here's a wonderful cardigan that is fun to crochet and beautiful to wear. It looks more difficult than it is, which is always nice.

SIZES
One size

FINISHED MEASUREMENTS
Length: 26 in / 66 cm
Chest: 44 in / 112 cm
Sleeve length: 17¼ in / 44 cm

MATERIALS
Yarn: (CYCA #3) Rowan Purelife British Sheep Breeds DK (100% wool; 131 yd/120 m / 50 g) and (CYCA #1) Rowan Fine Tweed (100% wool; 98 yd/90 m / 25 g)
Yarn Amounts: 23 balls Purelife Gray (Color A), 1 ball Fine Tweed Bell Busk #376 (Color B)
Hook: U.S. size G-6 / 4 mm

GAUGE
24 sts and 14 rows in pattern with larger hook = 4 x 4 in / 10 x 10 cm. Adjust hook size to obtain correct gauge if necessary.

PATTERNS
The edges are worked with Two-Color Knot Stripes (see page 64). The main pattern is Groups with Single and Double Crochet (see page 42).

BACK
With Color A, ch 123. Work the Two-Color Knot Stripes (see above), repeating Rows 2-5 twice and then Rows 2 and 3 once more; turn each row with ch 3. The border should now measure approx. 3¼ in / 8 cm.

Now work an eyelet pattern as follows:
Row 1: Ch 3 (= 1 dc) in 1st st, skip 2 sts, *ch 1 rather loosely, 2 dc in next st, skip 2 sts; rep from * across, ending with 1 dc in last st, ch 2, turn.
Row 2: *2 hdc around ch, 1 hdc between dc; rep from * across, ending with 1 hdc in top of tch. Now work in main pattern, decreasing 1 st on the first row so that 120 sts rem. Continue in pattern until piece measures 26 in / 66 cm. Cut yarn and fasten off.

LEFT FRONT
With Color A, ch 62 and work Knot Stripes, eyelet, and main pattern as for back until piece measures 8 in / 20 cm. Shape front neck by dec 1 st on every 6th row until 29 sts rem. Continue without further shaping until front is same length as back.

RIGHT FRONT
Work as for left front, reversing shaping.

SLEEVES
With Color A, ch 62 and work Knot Stripes as for left front. Begin main pattern and, *at the same time*, inc 1 st at each side on every 4th row until there are 90 sts. Continue without further shaping until sleeve is 17¼ in / 44 cm long or desired length. Cut yarn and fasten off.

FINISHING
Weave in all ends neatly on WS. Block pieces to finished measurements. Lay a damp towel over pieces or spray with water; leave until completely dry. Seam shoulders.

Front Band: Work 2 rows sc around front bands and neck—approx. 300 sts. Work an Eyelet pattern and then Knot Stripes as before but, *at the same time*, dec 2 sts over each shoulder on every row 7 times (each dec = 3 sc tog).

Final Steps: Attach sleeves, making sure that center of each sleeve matches shoulder seam. Sew side and sleeve seams. Lightly steam press seams under a damp pressing cloth.

This jacket's pattern shows up best in light colors.

Dress with Stand-Up Collar

The color choice is very important for the look of this dress. In black, you'll have a cocktail dress that will make you the center of attention at a party. Earth colors make it a pretty garment for any occasion.

SIZES
S (M, L)

FINISHED MEASUREMENTS
Length: 22 (22¾, 23¾) in / 82 (86, 90) cm
Chest: 31½ (35½, 39½) in / 80 (90, 100) cm
Hips: 32¼ (36¼, 40¼) in / 82 (92, 102) cm
Sleeve length: 5½ (6, 6¼) in / 14 (15, 16) cm

MATERIALS
Yarn: (CYCA #2), Schachenmayr Catania Solids (100% cotton; 137 yd/125 m / 50 g)
Yarn Amounts: 12 (13, 14) balls Hyacinth #240
Hook: U.S. size D-3 / 3.5 mm

GAUGE
25 sts and 21 rows in basic pattern = 4 x 4 in / 10 x 10 cm.
Adjust hook size to obtain correct gauge if necessary.

BASIC PATTERN
Row 1: Ch 4 (= 1 dc + ch 1), skip 2 sts, 1 dc in next st, *ch 1, skip 1 st, 1 dc in next st; rep from * across, with last st in top of tch; turn.
Row 2: Ch 3, skip 1st ch loop, 1 dc in next ch loop, go back and work 1 dc in skipped st (= crossed dc), *1 dc in next (empty) ch loop, go back and work 1 in in previous ch loop; rep from * to last ch loop, 1 dc in tch; turn (= the crossed dc encompasses the dc of previous row).
Row 3: Ch 1, 1 sc in 1st st, sc across with 1 sc in tch; turn.
Repeat Rows 1-3.

Panel A
Work Lace Square—Variation (see page 53).

Panel B
Foundation Row: Work dc across.
Then work Open Blocks (see page 54).

Panel C
Row 1: Ch 3, skip 1st st, 2 dc, ch 1, *3 dc, ch 1; rep from * across, ending with 3 dc; turn.
Row 2: Ch 4, *1 sc in ch loop, ch 3; rep from * to last st and end with 1 sc in top of tch; turn.
Repeat Rows 1 and 2.

BACK
Ch 131 (141, 151). Beginning in 2nd ch from hook, work 4 rows sc = 130 (140, 150) sc. Turn every row with ch 1.
Now work in Basic Pattern for 4 (4¼, 4¼) in / 10 (11, 11) cm. Next, work 2 rows hdc, then 6 rows Panel A, followed by 2 rows hdc. Work in Basic Pattern for 3½ (4, 4) in / 9 (10, 10) cm, decreasing 1 st at each side on every 4th row 6 times = 118 (128, 138) sts rem. Work 2 rows in hdc and then 5 rows Panel B (there should be 5 open blocks in length), and end with 2 rows hdc, decreasing 1 st at each side on the last row = 116 (126, 136) sts rem.

Now work in Basic Pattern for 3½ in / 9 cm, decreasing 1 st at each side on every 4th row until 92 (102, 112) sts rem. Work 2 rows in hdc and then 9 rows in Panel C. Place a marker at each side in the center row of Panel C = waist. The piece should now measure approx. 17¾ (18¼, 18¼) in / 45 (46, 46) cm. Work 2 rows hdc and then work the rest of the back in Basic Pattern, increasing 1 st at each side on every 6th row 4 times = 100 (110, 120) sts.

Continue without further shaping until piece measures 8¼ (8¾, 9) in / 21 (22, 23) cm from marker at waist.

Armholes: Sl st over the 1st 5 sts of row and then work in pattern to the last 5 sts; turn = 90 (100, 110) sts.

Now dec 1 st at each side on every other row 4 times = 82 (92, 102) sts rem. Continue without shaping until armhole measures 6¾ (7½, 8¼) in / 17 (19, 21) cm. Leave the center 46 sts unworked for neck and work each side separately. Work 2 rows over the 18 (20, 22) sts at each side. Cut yarn and fasten off.

FRONT

Work as for back until armhole measures 5¼ (5½, 6) in / 13 (14, 15) cm. Leave the center 36 sts unworked for neck. Work each side separately. Decrease 1 st on every row at neck edge until 18 (20, 22) sts rem. Continue until armhole is same length as on back. Cut yarn and fasten off. Work the other side of neck the same way, reversing shaping.

SLEEVES

Ch 73 (75, 77). Beginning in 2nd ch from hook, work 4 rows sc = 72 (74, 76) sc. Change to Basic Pattern and, *at the same time*, inc 1 st at each side on every other row to 84 (86, 90) sts. Continue in pattern until sleeve is approx. 5½ (6¼, 7) in / 14 (16, 18) cm long, ending on same pattern row as last row before armhole on front/back.

Sleeve Cap: Sl st over 1st 5 sts, work in pattern to last 5 sts; turn = 74 (76, 80) sts rem. Now decrease 1 st at each side on every row until 58 (60, 62) sts rem. Next, *sl st over the 1st 4 sts, work to last 4 sts; turn; rep from * 2 more times. Cut yarn and fasten off.

FINISHING

Weave in all ends neatly on WS. Steam press all the pieces on WS under a damp pressing cloth; or block pieces to finished measurements, spray with water, and leave until completely dry. Join shoulders.

Collar: Begin at one shoulder and work around neck. Ch 2 (= 1 hdc), work in hdc with approx. 58 (60, 62) hdc for back neck and approx. 80 (82, 84) hdc for front neck = 138 (142, 146) sts total. Work back and forth in hdc, ending every row with 1 sl

A red or black slip will also work nicely.

st in the top of tch; turn. Begin next row with ch 2 (tch). Count out from the shoulder and inc 1 st by working 2 hdc into the same st, inc with 3 sts between a total of 3 times in each side of shoulder = 12 sts increased. Work another 3 rows and inc 1 st at each shoulder on every row = 6 sts increased and a total of 156 (160, 164) sts. Now work 6 rows in Panel B, *at the same time* increasing 3 (5, 7) sts on the 1st row; end with 1 sl st in 1st ch;

turn. End with ch 2, *1 hdc, ch 1, skip 1 st; rep from * to last st and end with 1 sl st in the top of tch. Cut yarn and fasten off.

Final steps: Sew side and sleeve seams. Attach sleeves. Lightly steam press seams. Weave in any loose ends.

Chevron Pattern Shawl

You can own as many shawls as you like and it really won't be enough. A pretty shawl in the right colors transforms the simplest outfit into something special.

FINISHED MEASUREMENTS

59 x 15¾ in / 150 x 40 cm (excluding fringe)

MATERIALS

Yarn: (CYCA #0), Rowan Kid Silk Haze (70% mohair, 30% silk; 229 yd/210 m / 25 g) and Anchor Artisté Metallic (80% viscose, 20% polyester; 109 yd/100 m / 25 g)

Yarn Amounts: 15-25 g of each color. We used small amounts in the following colors: beige, gray, gray-blue, light gray, warm gray, light purple, gray-purple, pink, wine red, cerise, cyclamen, red, orange, gray-pink, ice blue, turquoise, olive green, dark green, and yellow. We also used small amounts of metallic yarn in the following colors: light blue, gold, wine red, copper.

Hook: U.S. size H-8 / 5 mm

GAUGE

18 sts and 7 rows in pattern with yarn held double = approx. 4 x 4 in / 10 x 10 cm.

Adjust hook size to obtain correct gauge if necessary.

Work with the Silk Haze yarn held double and the Metallic as a single strand. The pattern is double crochet except for the Metallic rows, which are worked in half double crochet. Leave approx. 9¾ in / 25 cm of yarn at each side when you change yarns for the fringe.

The shawl is worked across the width in the Simple Chevron pattern (see page 55). Holding 2 strands of olive green together, ch 223. Work the first 2 rows in pattern with olive green. Continue in stripes as follows: 1 row yellow, 1 row gold Metallic (in hdc), 2 rows beige, 1 row gray, 1 row gray-blue, 1 row light blue Metallic (in hdc), 2 rows light gray, 1 row light purple, 1 row gray-purple, 2 rows pink, 1 row wine red, 1 row wine red Metallic (in hdc), 1 row cyclamen, 2 rows red, 1 row cerise, 1 row orange, 1 row copper Metallic (hdc), 1 row gray-pink, 1 row gray-purple, 2 rows warm gray, 1 row light blue Metallic (hdc), 1 row ice blue, 2 rows turquoise, 1 row dark green, 1 row beige, 2 rows yellow.

FINISHING

Pin out shawl to finished measurements, spray with water, and leave until completely dry. Cut 20 in / 50 cm lengths of Silk Haze and knot fringe, with 4 strands in each bundle, also tying in the strands on the short sides. Tie on fringe in the same color as the row each is attached to.

Slippers

Function marries feeling with these beautiful slippers. They are no more slippery than regular socks and much cozier.

SIZES
S (M, L) = women's shoe sizes U.S. 5-6 (7-8, 9-10) / European 36 (38, 40)

MATERIALS
Yarn: (CYCA #3), Schachenmayr Cotton Time (100% cotton; 96 yd/88 m / 50 g)
Yarn Amounts: 3 (3, 3) balls Gray #98 (MC) and 1 (1, 1) ball White #01 (CC)
Hook: U.S. sizes G-6 / 4 mm

GAUGE
18 sts and 20 rows in sc in the round = 4 x 4 in / 10 x 10 cm.
Adjust hook size to obtain correct gauge if necessary.

Make 2 slippers alike.

SOLE
With MC, ch 25. Work the sole in the round as follows:
Rnd 1: Insert hook into 2nd ch from hook and work 5 sc into that ch, work 22 sc with 1 sc each into next 22 ch, 5 sc in last ch and then work 22 sc across other side of foundation ch. End this and all following rnds with 1 sl st into 1st sc. Begin each rnd with ch 1.
Rnd 2: Mark the center st of each short side. *Work in sc around to marked st, 5 sc in that st; rep from * once more.
Repeat Rnd 2—3 (4, 5) times.
Next rnd: Work around in sc with 1 sc in each st (no increasing). Work this rnd 2 (3, 4) times total.

FOOT
Make 5 squares in the following color sequence: Rnd 1: MC, Rnd 2: CC, Rnds 3 and 4: MC.
Ch 4 and join into a ring with sl st.
Rnd 1: Ch 3 (= 1st dc), 3 dc around ch ring, ch 1; rep from * 2 more times, 1 sl st into top of beg ch. Change color.

Begin all rnds at a corner stitch and end with 1 sl st into top of beg ch; cut yarn and fasten off. Change to a new color at end of every round.
Rnd 2: (Ch 3, 3 dc, ch 1 and 4 dc) in corner, ch 1, *(4 dc, ch 1, 4 dc) in corner, ch 1; rep from * 2 more times.
Rnd 3: Work 1 dc in each st around and (1 dc, 5-dc cluster, 1 dc) in each corner.
Rnd 4: Work 1 sc in each st around.
For size L, work another rnd of sc to make the squares slightly larger.

FINISHING
Sew the squares together, working through back loops only for a visible ridge. First, join 4 squares into a strip. Place the last square diagonally against the others and sew the short sides of the strip so that tip of last square points up to instep and the two free sides face toe. Sew foot down around sole.
Heel loop: With MC, ch 10 between the 2 back squares and then work back with 1 sc in each ch. Finish with crab stitch

(see page 71) all around,
including the loop.

Decorative Flower (make 2 alike):
With MC, ch 13, and, beginning in
3rd ch from hook, work 3 dc in
each ch. Swirl strip around into a
flower shape and sew securely to
center front of slipper.

This photo shows two versions of the
slippers. The instructions are for the
left slipper (at top in photo) but you
can also make slippers with granny
squares (see page 78) as in the right
slipper (at bottom).

Envelope Bag and Smart Phone Cover

Beads add a magic touch to many items. This easy set, with a smart phone cover and bag, is completely transformed by glittering beads.

FINISHED MEASUREMENTS

Bag: 6 in / 15 cm long and 9¾ in / 25 cm wide, 1 in / 2.5 cm deep
Cover: 4¾ in / 12 cm long, 2¾ in / 7 cm wide

MATERIALS

Yarn: (CYCA #1), Rowan Siena 4 ply (100% cotton; 153 yd/140 m / 50 g)
Yarn Amounts: 3 balls Beacon #668
Hook: U.S. size D-3 / 3 mm
Beads: approx. 350 glass seed beads size 8/0 (or size to fit over doubled strand of yarn) + beading needle
Notions: magnetic lock for bag

GAUGE

36 sts and 24 rows in pattern = 4 x 4 in / 10 x 10 cm.
25 sts and 28 rows in sc = 4 x 4 in / 10 x 10 cm.
Adjust hook size to obtain correct gauge if necessary.

Bead Crochet: see page 73.

ENVELOPE BAG

Back and Front are worked in one piece. Ch 63. Beginning in 2nd ch from hook, work Groups with Single and Double Crochet pattern (see page 42) until piece is 14½ in / 37 cm long. Cut yarn and fasten off.
Mark down 6 in / 15 cm from the 1st row and then ⅝ in / 1.5 cm in on each side of the marker = bottom of bag.
Side strips (make 2 alike): Ch 9 and then, beginning in 2nd ch from hook, work in sc until strip is 5¼ in / 13 cm long. Turn each row with ch 1. Cut yarn and fasten off.
Strap: String 200 beads onto yarn. Ch 17. Beginning in 2nd ch from hook, work in sc without beads for 2½ in / 6 cm. Now continue in sc, adding in beads as follows:
Row 1 (WS): *1 sc, bring up bead so it lies on back of work, 1 sc; rep from * across, ending with 1 sc; turn.
Row 2: Work across in sc without beads.
Repeat Rows 1 and 2 until strap measures a total of 7 in / 18 cm (= 14 bead rows). Cut yarn and fasten off.

FINISHING

Weave in all yarn ends neatly on WS. Steam press the pieces under a damp pressing cloth, or spray with water, and leave until completely dry.
Match the short ends of side strips with the bottom markers on the front and back and sew together. Next, seam the long sides of the strip to the bag.
Make a small pleat at top of short sides and secure with a couple of stitches.
Place the strap at the center of the back, 4¼ in / 11 cm from the bottom. Securely sew the part of the strap without beads to back of bag. Let the other side hang loose. Sew one part of the magnetic lock under the strap

front and the other to front of bag.

SMART PHONE COVER
Back and Front (make 2 alike):
Ch 21 and work in same pattern as for bag for 4¼ in / 11 cm. Cut yarn and fasten off.

Seam the sides and bottom. Work 4 rounds of sc around the top edge.

Cord: String 150 beads. Work a foundation chain, and *at the same time*, place beads: bring up 1 bead and lay it behind the ch, work next ch. Continue alternating beads and ch sts until cord is approx. 23½ in / 60 cm long or desired length. Cut yarn and fasten off.

FINISHING
Weave in all yarn ends neatly on WS. Lightly steam press the pieces under a damp pressing cloth, or spray with water, and leave until completely dry. Securely sew beaded cord to top of cover.

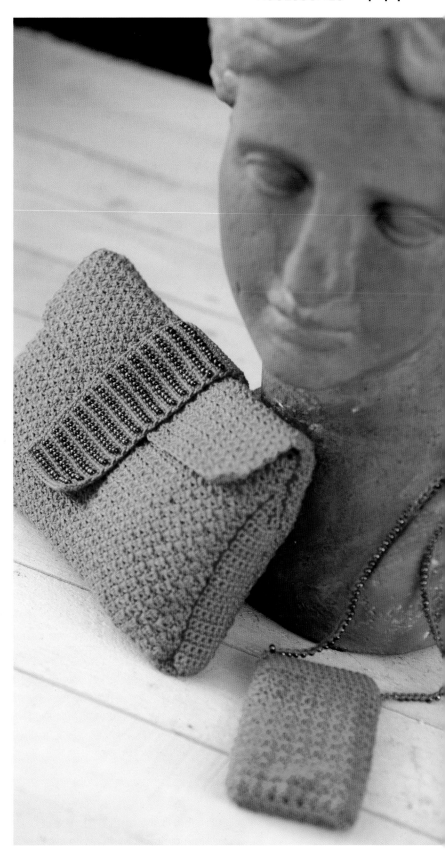

Hat and Half Gloves

Wearing matching mittens and a hat is an easy way to look well-dressed. Soft earth colors give an elegant and sleek impression while the same set in scarlet, pink, or lime green is much sportier.

HAT

SIZE
One size

FINISHED MEASUREMENTS
Circumference: approx. 22 in / 56 cm

MATERIALS
Yarn: (CYCA #4), Rowan Alpaca Cotton (72% alpaca, 28% cotton; 148 yd/135 m / 50 g)
Yarn Amounts: 1 ball Raindrop #404
Hook: U.S. size M/N-13 / 9 mm

GAUGE
10 sts and 5 rows in pattern = 4 x 4 in / 10 x 10 cm.
Adjust hook size to obtain correct gauge if necessary.

HALF GLOVES

SIZE
One size

FINISHED MEASUREMENTS
Length: 8 in / 20 cm
Circumference: approx. 8 in / 20 cm

MATERIALS
Yarn: (CYCA #4), Rowan Alpaca Cotton (72% alpaca, 28% cotton; 148 yd/135 m / 50 g)
Yarn Amounts: 1 ball Raindrop #404
Hook: U.S. size H-8 / 5 mm

GAUGE
14 sts and 10 rows in pattern = 4 x 4 in / 10 x 10 cm.
Adjust hook size to obtain correct gauge if necessary.

HAT
Hold yarn double throughout. Ch 5 and join into a ring with 1 sl st.

Rnd 1: Ch 1 (does *not* count as 1 sc), 12 sc around ring, 1 sl st into 1st ch = 12 sc.

Rnd 2: Ch 1 (does *not* count as 1 sc), 1 sc, ch 1, (1 sc in next st, ch 1) 11 times, and end with 1 sl st into 1st ch = 24 sc.

Rnd 3: Ch 4 (= 1 dc + ch 1), skip 1st sc, 1 dc in next ch, work (1 dc, ch 1, 1 dc) in each ch around, ending with 1 sl st into 3rd st of beg ch = 36 sts.

Rnd 4: Sl st to the 1st ch, ch 4 (= 1 dc + ch 1), 1 dc in same ch, *ch 1, (1 dc, ch 1, 1 dc) in next ch; rep from * around, ch 1, 1 sl st in 3rd st of beg ch = 48 sts.

Rnd 5: Sl st to the 1st ch, ch 4 (= 1 dc + ch 1), 1 dc in same ch, *ch 2, (1 dc, ch 1, 1 dc) in next ch; rep from * around, ending with ch 2, 1 sl st in 3rd st of beg ch = 57 sts.

Rnd 6: Sl st to the 1st ch, ch 3 (= 1 dc), 1 dc, ch 1 and 2 dc in same ch loop, *skip 4 dc, 2 dc, ch 1 and 2 dc in next ch loop; rep from * around, ending with

1 sl st into 1st ch.
Rnds 7-10: Work as for Rnd 6. Cut yarn and fasten off.

FINISHING
Weave in all yarn ends neatly on WS. Lightly steam press hat on WS under a damp pressing cloth or spray with water, and leave until completely dry.

HALF GLOVES
Both gloves are worked alike using a single strand of yarn throughout.

Cuff: Ch 16. Beginning in 2nd ch from hook, work back and forth in sc through back loops until piece is 6¾ in / 17 cm long. Turn each row with ch 1. Crochet short ends together to form a ring.

Hand: Begin at one side of ring. Begin with 1 rnd sc with 1 st in each row around. End every rnd with 1 sl st to join. Work around in V-stitch Double Crochet pattern (see page 42) for 9 rnds or to desired length to thumbhole.

Thumbhole: Work around in pattern but skip 1 pattern

repeat at beginning of rnd and ch 3 over gap, insert hook into the 4th st and continue around. On the next rnd, work 1 repeat of the V-shaped dc in the center ch. Work another 2 rnds and then work 1 rnd in sc.

Fan edge: *1 sc, skip 2 sts, 5 dc in same st, skip 2 sts; rep from * around, ending with 1 sl st in the 1st sc. Cut yarn and fasten off.

FINISHING

Weave in all yarn ends neatly on WS. Lightly steam press half gloves on WS under a damp pressing cloth, or spray with water, and leave until completely dry.

String Bag

A practical bag that can replace your handbag every now and then. It's easy to crochet, so it's even more enticing.

FINISHED MEASUREMENTS
Length: approx. 31½ in / 80 cm, including shoulder strap
Circumference: 17¼ in / 44 cm

MATERIALS
Yarn: (CYCA #2), sportweight 2-ply natural 100% linen cord (approx. 284 yd/260 m / skein)
Yarn Amounts: 2 skeins
Hook: U.S. size 7 / 4.5 mm

GAUGE
20 sts and 11 rows in pattern = 4 x 4 in / 10 x 10 cm.
Adjust hook size to obtain correct gauge if necessary.

BAG
Ch 4 and join into a ring with 1 sl st.

NOTE Begin every rnd with ch 3 (= 1 hdc + ch 1).

Rnd 1: Ch 3, (1 hdc around ring, ch 1) 7 times, 1 sl st into 2nd st of beg ch; turn = 8 ch loops.
Rnd 2: 1 sl st in the 1st ch loop, ch 3, 1 hdc into same loop (that is, the 1st loop), *ch 1, (1 hdc, ch 1, 1 hdc) in next ch loop; rep from * and end with ch 1, 1 sl st into 2nd st of beg ch; turn = 16 ch loops.
Rnd 3: 1 sl st into 1st ch loop, ch 3, 1 dc in same ch loop, *ch 1, 1 hdc into next ch loop, ch 1**, (1 hdc, ch 1 and 1 hdc) into next ch loop; rep from * around, ending last rep at **. 1 sl st into 2nd st of beg ch; turn = 25 ch loops.
Rnd 4: 1 sl st into 1st ch loop, ch 3, 1 hdc into same loop, *(ch 1, 1 hdc in next ch loop) 2 times, ch 1**, 1 hdc, (ch 1 and 1 hdc) in next ch loop; rep from *, ending last rep at **. 1 sl st into 2nd st of beg ch; turn = 32 ch loops.
Rnd 5: 1 sl st into 1st ch loop, ch 3, 1 hdc into same loop, *(ch 1, 1 hdc in next ch loop) 3 times, ch 1**, 1 hdc, (ch 1 and 1 hdc) in next ch loop; rep from *, ending last rep at **. 1 sl st into 2nd st of beg ch; turn = 40 ch loops.
Continue working as set, increasing as on Rnd 5 until there are 78 ch loops.
Now work without increasing for 25 rnds. The bag should now measure approx. 14¼ in / 36 cm from the 1st rnd.

HANDLE
Divide the work in half, placing a marker at each side. Work each side separately. Work in hdc and ch as set in rows back and forth. *At the same time,* decrease 1 st at each side on every row until 6 ch-groups rem. Work for 20 rows or to desired length without further shaping.
Make the other side the same way. Crochet the handle pieces together on the last row. Weave in all ends neatly on WS.

This bag is pretty and practical no matter what color you choose for it.

Scarf in Pastel Tones

You couldn't find a multi-color scarf easier to crochet than this. These days there are so many yarns dyed with several colors that you can choose a color scheme you like and create something that looks quite difficult with almost no effort at all.

FINISHED MEASUREMENTS
13¾ x 65 in / 35 x 165 cm

MATERIALS
Yarn: (CYCA #4), Colinette Mohair hand-dyed (73% mohair, 22% wool, 5% nylon; 102 yd/93 m / 50 g)
Yarn Amounts: 3 skeins Pink Tweed
Hook: U.S. size J-10 / 6 mm

GAUGE
10 sts and 6 rows in pattern = 4 x 4 in / 10 x 10 cm.
Adjust hook size to obtain correct gauge if necessary.

INSTRUCTIONS
Ch 34 + 2 and work in V-stitch Double Crochet (see page 42) until scarf measures approx. 65 in / 165 cm or desired length.

FINISHING
Fringe: Cut lengths of yarn approx. 8 in / 20 cm long. Knot a group of 4 strands into every 3rd st. Trim fringe even.

Of course, you can also crochet this scarf in a solid color.

Snood

Snoods are so warm and can be worn by both men and women. They are practical and cozy and many people prefer them to scarves.

FINISHED MEASUREMENTS
Width: 12¾ in / 32 cm
Circumference: approx. 63 in / 160 cm

MATERIALS
Yarn: (CYCA #4), Rowan Alpaca Cotton (72% alpaca, 28% cotton; 148 yd/135 m / 50 g)
Yarn Amounts: 3 balls Raindrop #404
Hook: U.S. size J-10 / 6 mm

GAUGE
14 sts and 6 rows in pattern = 4 x 4 in / 10 x 10 cm.
Adjust hook size to obtain correct gauge if necessary.

Ch 36 and, beginning in 4th ch from hook, work in Deep Spike Double Crochet pattern (see page 65).

Work in pattern until piece is 63 in / 160 cm long. Crochet the short ends together with sl sts (do not work sts too tightly).

FINISHING
Weave in all ends neatly on WS. Work 1 rnd sc around both outer edges and then make a fan edging as follows: *1 sc, skip 2 sts, work 5 dc in next st, skip 2 sts; rep from * around, ending with 1 sl st into 1st sc. Cut yarn and fasten off.

Lightly steam press snood under a damp pressing cloth, or spray with water, and leave until completely dry.

Tie

Crocheted ties were very stylish in the 1970s. Fashion goes in cycles, and, sure enough, they are once again in style.

FINISHED MEASUREMENTS
Width across front: 2½ in / 6 cm
Length: 55 in / 140 cm

MATERIALS
Yarn: (CYCA #1), Rowan Fine Tweed (100% wool; 98 yd/90 m / 25 g)
Yarn Amounts: 2 balls Askrigg #365 (Color A) and 1 ball Tissington #386 (Color B)
Hook: U.S. size D-3 / 3 mm

GAUGE
12 sts and 12 rows in pattern = 2 x 2 in / 5 x 5 cm Adjust hook size to obtain correct gauge if necessary.

PATTERN
Multiple of 3 sts + 2.
Row 1: Skip 2 ch (= 1 sc), *work (1 sc, ch 1, 1 sc) in next ch, skip 2 ch; rep from * across and end with 1 sc in last ch; turn.
Row 2: Ch 1 (= 1 sc), *(1 sc, ch 1, 1 sc) in next ch; rep from * across, ending with 1 sc in tch.
Repeat Row 2 throughout.

TIE
With Color A, ch 16. Beginning in 3rd ch from hook, work across in pattern = 14 sts. Work 17 pattern rows and then continue in pattern in the following color sequence:
*2 rows Color B, 2 rows Color A, 2 rows B, 2 rows A, 2 rows B, 16 rows Color A; rep from * another 2 times. Work the rest of the tie with Color A, continuing in pattern until piece is 26½ in / 67 cm long. Now work in hdc, decreasing 1 st at each side on every row 3 times = 8 sts rem. When narrow strip is 1¾ in / 30 cm long, increase 1 st at each side 2 times = 12 sts. Work without further shaping until tie is 55 in / 140 cm long. Cut yarn and fasten off.

FINISHING
Tie loop on the back: Attach loop to center Color B stripe as follows: With Color B, beginning inside the outermost st, ch 8, insert hook inside the outermost stitch on the opposite side of color stripe and work 1 st sl in each ch; fasten off yarn.
Blocking: Lightly steam press the tie on the WS under a damp pressing cloth, or spray with water. Leave until completely dry.

Turquoise Hat

The soft alpaca yarn makes this hat light, warm, and beautiful.

SIZE
One size

FINISHED MEASUREMENTS
Circumference: approx. 21¼ in / 54 cm

MATERIALS
Yarn: (CYCA #3-4) Kinna Textiles Alpaca/Silk (60% alpaca, 10% silk, 30% Merino wool; approx. 125 yd/115 m / 50 g)
Yarn Amounts: 2 skeins Turquoise #1590
Hook: U.S. sizes G-6 and J-10 / 4 and 6 mm

GAUGE
12 sts and 8 rows in dc pattern with doubled yarn on larger hook = 4 x 4 in / 10 x 10 cm.
Adjust hook sizes to obtain correct gauge if necessary.

Hold yarn double throughout. With larger hook, ch 6 and join into a ring with 1 sl st. Begin each rnd with ch 3 and end with 1 sl st into top of 3 ch. Work 7 rnds in dc to shape crown as follows:

Rnd 1: Ch 3 (= 1 dc), work 9 dc around ring = 10 dc. End with 1 sl st into top of beg ch.

Rnd 2: Work 2 dc in each st = 20 dc.

Rnd 3: Work 2 dc in every other st = 30 dc.

Rnd 4: Work as for Rnd 3 = 45 dc.

Rnd 5: Work 2 dc in every 3rd st = 60 dc.

Rnd 6: Work 2 dc in every 4th st = 75 dc.

Rnd 7: Work in dc around without increasing.
Now begin pattern rounds, turning at end of each round.

Rnd 8: Ch 3 (= 1 dc), work around in dc, ending with 1 sl st into top of beg ch; turn.

Rnd 9: Ch 2, 3 hdc, *ch 1, 5 dc tog (= bobble), ch 1, 5 hdc; rep from * to last 2 sts and end with 2 hdc, 1 sl st into top of beg ch; turn.

Rnds 10-12: Work as for Rnd 8, with 1 dc over each chain st and bobble so that the stitch count remains constant.

Rnd 13: Work as for Rnd 9.

Rnds 14-17: Work as for Rnd 8. Change to smaller hook and finish with 3 rnds Front and Back Post Double Crochet alternating in front of and behind work (see page 62).

Rnd 18: Ch 3, *FPdc, BPdc; rep from * around, ending with 1 sl st into top of beg ch.

Rnds 19 and 20: Work as for Rnd 18 with FPdc over FPdc and BPdc over BPdc so that the pattern looks like ribbing.
Cut yarn and fasten off.

The hat and this scarf (see page 138) match beautifully even though they were made with different yarns and stitches. The turquoise ties them together. →

Bag and Clutch

This bag is easy to change. Remove the button and strap for a cute tote bag, or add some beads and a handle to raise the level of elegance.

FINISHED MEASUREMENTS

Bag: 15 in / 38 cm long and 17¼ in / 44 cm wide
Clutch: 5½ in / 14 cm long and 8 in / 20 cm wide

MATERIALS

Yarn: (CYCA #4), Rowan Original Denim (100% cotton; 100 yd/91 m / 50 g)
Yarn Amounts: 7 balls Ecru #324 (shown)
Notions: 1 shank button for bag, approx. 1¾ in / 4.5 cm diameter; an 8 in / 20 cm long zipper for clutch
Hook: U.S. sizes G-6 / 4 mm

GAUGE

28 sts and 17 rows in pattern = 4 x 4 in / 10 x 10 cm.
18 sts and 22 rows in sc = 4 x 4 in / 10 x 10 cm. Adjust hook size to obtain correct gauge if necessary.

PATTERNS

Foundation Rnd: Work 1 hdc in each st with ch 1 between each hdc. The 1st hdc of the row is worked as ch 2; end row with 1 sl st into top of beg ch.
Pattern Rnd: *1 hdc in ch of previous rnd, ch 1; rep from * around.
Repeat Pattern Rnd throughout.
Crab st: sc worked backwards (see page 71).

BAG

The bag is worked in the round.
Bottom: Ch 45. Beginning in 2nd ch from hook, work in sc to last st of foundation chain, work 3 sc in last st and then work in sc across other side of foundation ch, with 2 sc in same st as 1st ch, end with 1 sl st into 1st st. Place a marker at the center of each of the groups of 3 sc at each end. Work ch 1 at beginning of each rnd and 1 sl st into 1st sc at end. Work around in sc, increasing with 3 sc in each of the 3 sts at short ends (the marked st + 1 st on each side of marked st). Increase the same way on each rnd with 1 st more between increases. Stop increasing when there are 5 sts between increases. Now work

around without shaping until the bottom is 2¾ in / 7 cm as measured out from the foundation chain.
Sides: Continue working around but change to pattern, beginning with foundation row. Work 9½ in / 24 cm in pattern.
Top Edge: Mark the center back and center front of bag. Make a pleat 6 sts wide by overlapping 3 sts over 3 sts at the center. Pin or baste the pleat. Work in sc. On the 1st rnd, work 1 sc in each ch and hdc of previous rnd, working through both layers of the pleat to join it. Continue around in sc until edging measures 2½ in / 6 cm. Finish with 1 rnd crab st.
Handle (make 2 alike): Make a chain approx. 19¾ in / 50 cm long or desired length. Work as for bottom of bag but increase with 3 sc in the center st of every rnd a total of 3 times. End with 1 rnd crab st.
Button: Make a slip knot and work 8 sc around loop; pull loop tight so there is no hole. Work around with 2 sc in each st on the 1st rnd. On subsequent rnds, work in sc with 1 st more between increases until the circle is slightly smaller than the

button. Place the button inside the circle and crochet a couple of rounds without increasing. Leaving a long tail, sew basting stitches through the outer edge of the circle. Pull tight; save the yarn tail to sew on the button. Place the button at the center of one of the pleats and sew it down securely.

Button Loop: Ch 23 and then work in hdc down one side of the chain. Ch 16-18 (make sure the button fits through the ch loop) and then work in hdc

down opposite side of foundation chain. Work in crab st around. Sew the loop to side of bag opposite button.

Sew the handles on approx. 3¼ in / 8 cm from each side of the pleat, with base of handle on 1st round of sc edging.

TIPS & TRICKS

If you want a shorter bag than the one shown, work fewer rounds in the pattern. This changes the bag's proportions so it will look shorter and wider.

If instead you want a narrower bag, make fewer increases before you work the rest of the bag.

CLUTCH

Ch 36 and work the 1st rnd as for base of bag. Continue working around without increasing until the piece measures 5½ in / 14 cm from foundation chain. Finish with 1 rnd crab st. Sew in the zipper inside edging.

SIZES
One size

FINISHED MEASUREMENTS
Length: 7 in / 18 cm
Circumference: 8 in / 20 cm

MATERIALS
Yarn: (CYCA #4), Rowan Purelife Renew (93% wool, 7% nylon; 82 yd/75 m / 50 g)
Yarn Amounts: 2 balls Diesel #685
Hook: U.S. sizes H-8 / 5 mm

GAUGE
14 sts and 8 rows in dc = 4 x 4 in / 10 x 10 cm. Adjust hook size to obtain correct gauge if necessary.

Half Gloves in Thick Wool

Warm and pretty half gloves for anyone who needs their fingers free when it's cold outside. They also provide warm protection for tender wrists and hands.

Make both gloves alike.

Ch 24 and join into a ring with 1 sl st. Work around in dc, beginning each rnd with ch 3 (= 1 dc). End each rnd with 1 sl st into top of beg ch. Work 10 rnds in dc or to desired length to thumbhole.
Thumbhole: Continue as set but, at beginning of next rnd, skip 3 sts, ch 3, insert hook into 4th st and continue in dc around. On the next rnd, work 3 dc around the ch-3 loop. Work 3 more ends.
Picot Edging: Work 1 sc, *ch 3, 1 sl st into 1st ch, 2 sc; rep from * around, ending with 1 sl st into 1st sc. Cut yarn and fasten off.

FINISHING
Weave in all ends neatly on WS. Lightly steam press the half gloves on the WS under a damp pressing cloth, or spray with water. Leave until completely dry.

Triangular Mohair Shawl

The color choice makes this shawl. The same shawl in pale tone-on-tone colors produces a much softer impression. With black and a couple of shades of gray, it will be quite elegant.

FINISHED MEASUREMENTS
Long side: 75 in / 190 cm
Short sides: 49¼ in / 125 cm

MATERIALS
Yarn: (CYCA #0), Rowan Kid Silk Haze (70% mohair, 30% silk; 229 yd/210 m / 50 g)
Yarn Amounts: 5 balls Splendor #579 (MC), 1 ball each Marmalade #596, Candy Girl #606, and Grace #580
Hook: U.S. size G-6 / 4 mm

GAUGE
4 ch loops = approx. 4¼ in / 11 cm in width and 4 in / 10 cm in length. Adjust hook size to obtain correct gauge if necessary.

NOTE Hold yarn double throughout.

With MC, ch 7.
Row 1: Work 1 dc in 7th ch from hook; turn = 1st ch loop.
Row 2: Ch 7, (1 sc, ch 5, and 1 tr) in ch loop; turn = 2 ch loops.
Row 3: Ch 7, 1 sc in 1st ch loop, ch 5, (1 sc, ch 5, and 1 tr) in last ch loop; turn = 3 ch loops.
Row 4: Ch 7, 1 sc in 1st ch loop, ch 5, 1 sc in next ch loop, ch 5, (1 sc, ch 5, and 1 tr) in last ch loop; turn = 4 ch loops.
Row 5: Ch 7, 1 sc in 1st ch loop, ch 5, (1 sc in next ch loop, ch 5) 2 times, (1 sc, ch 5, and 1 tr) in last ch loop; turn = 5 ch loops.
Row 6: Ch 7, 1 sc in 1st ch loop, ch 5, (1 sc in next ch loop, ch 5) across and end with (1 sc, ch 5, and 1 tr) in last ch loop; turn = 6 ch loops.
Repeat Row 6 until there are 66 ch loops or shawl is desired size.

Edging along short sides:
Row 1: With Marmalade, work 1 dc, ch 1, 1 dc in 1st ch loop, ch 2, *1 dc, ch 1, 1 dc in next ch loop, ch 2*; rep from * to tip, work (1 dc, ch 1, 1 dc, ch 3, 1 dc, ch 1, 1 dc, ch 2) in tip; rep from * to * on opposite side of shawl, ending with 1 dc, ch 1, 1 dc in last ch loop.
Rows 2 and 3: Change to Candy Girl and work as for Row 1 but with ch 2 between each dc instead of ch 1 and work (1 dc, ch 2, 1 dc) in loop at tip.
Row 4: Change to Grace and work as for Row 3.
Row 5: Change to Marmalade and work as for Row 3.

FINISHING
Weave in all ends neatly on WS. Block shawl to finished measurements, making sure that the tip is centered. Place a damp towel over the shawl or spray shawl with water. Leave until completely dry.

A fun shawl that is quick to crochet.

Mittens and Hat

MITTENS

SIZES
Women's (Men's)

FINISHED MEASUREMENTS
Length (excluding cuff): 8¼ (9) in / 21 (23) cm
Circumference: 8 (8¾) in / 20 (22) cm

MATERIALS
Yarn: (CYCA #4), Rowan Kid Classic (70% wool, 22% mohair, 8% nylon; 153 yd/140 m / 50 g)
Yarn Amounts: 2 balls Kid Classic Crushed Velvet #825, small amount of finer CC yarn
Hook: U.S. sizes D-3 and 7 / 3 and 4.5 mm

GAUGE
10 sts and 12 rows in sc with larger hook = 2 x 2 in / 5 x 5 cm.
Adjust hook sizes to obtain correct gauge if necessary.

HAT

FINISHED MEASUREMENTS
Circumference: 20½ in / 52 cm

MATERIALS
Yarn: (CYCA #3), Rowan Pure Wool DK (100% wool; 136 yd/124 m / 50 g)
Yarn Amounts: 2 balls MC (Glade #021) and a small amount of CC yarn for pattern (Kiss #036)
Hook: U.S. size 7 / 4.5 mm

GAUGE
21 sts and 30 rows in sc = 4 x 4 in / 10 x 10 cm.
Adjust hook size to obtain correct gauge if necessary.

Mittens are firmer when crocheted in slip stitches—and lighter if worked in half double crochet.

LEFT MITTEN
Cuff: With larger hook and MC, ch 16 (18). Beginning in 2nd ch from hook, work 1 row sc = 15 (17) sc. Work back and forth in sc worked through back loops for "ribbing." Turn each row with ch 1 (which does *not* count as a sc). Work a total of 38 (42) rows or to desired length to fit around wrist. Crochet short ends together.

Hand: Ch 1, work 1 sc in each row = 38 (42) sc. Continue in sc, working around in a spiral (see page 18) until hand measures 2¾ (3¼) in / 7 (8) cm (or desired length to thumbhole) from the 1st circular round (all measurements are taken from this point). Use a thread to baste directly up from the cuff seam so that the marker is centered on the inside of the wrist.

Thumbhole: Work until 10 (11) sts before marker, ch 9 (10) and skip 9 (10) sts. On the next rnd, work 9 (10) sc in ch loop. Continue crocheting around in sc until mitten measures 7½ (8) in / 19 (20) cm or to tip of little finger. Place a marker at each side.

Shape top: Dec by working 2 sc tog on each side of each marker. Dec on every rnd 5 (6) times and then work 2 sc tog around until all the sts have been used. Pull the yarn tightly as you work or use a smaller size hook to avoid holes between the decreased stitches.

Thumb: With larger hook and MC, work 18 (20) sc around the thumbhole. Dec 2 sts on 1st

rnd (= dec 1 st at each side). Continue around in sc until thumb is 2½ (2¾) in / 6 (7) cm long or desired length. Dec 1 st at each side on every rnd 2 times and then 2 sc tog around until all the sts are used up.

Cuff Edging: With smaller hook and CC, work 1 sc in every other row and ch 3 after each sc.

RIGHT MITTEN

Work as for left mitten, placing thumbhole 1 (2) sts after marker.

TIPS & TRICKS

This is a good basic pattern. You can use whatever size yarn you like. Begin by crocheting the cuff long enough to fit around wrist, with fewer sts across for a shorter cuff or more sts for a longer one. Crochet the cuff together and then work 1 sc in each row, beginning at the seam. Make sure that the cuff goes over your hand. Use the same length measurements as given in the pattern but adjust the number of thumb stitches according to the size yarn: Finer yarn requires more thumbhole stitches and heavier yarn fewer. Adjust the number of rnds for shaping the top depending on whether you have more or fewer stitches than in the basic pattern.

HAT

With hook U.S. size 7 / 4.5 mm and MC, ch 5 and join into a

ring with 1 sl st. Work the hat in the round.

Foundation Rnd: Work 5 sc around ring, ending this and all following rnds with 1 sl st into 1st sc. Begin each rnd in 1st st after the sc that the sl st was worked into. Place a marker into 1st st to make it easy to see where the round begins.

Rnd 1: Work 2 sc in each st = 10 sc.

Rnd 2: Work 2 sc in 1st st, 1 sc in next st. Continue alternating 2 sc into 1 st and 1 sc into next around = 15 sc.

Rnd 3: Work 2 sc into 1st st, 1 sc each into next 2 sts. Continue alternating 2 sc into 1 st and then 1 sc into each of next 2 sts around = 20 sc.

Increase the same way, with 1 more st between increases, stacking increases over each other. Each rnd increases by 5 sts. Inc as set until there are 110

sts; remove marker.

Now work sc in a spiral (see page 18) without the sl st at beginning of rnd and without increasing. Continue around until hat measures 6 in / 15 cm from top, working 2 sc tog at each side on last rnd = 108 sts. Now begin the blocks which are 3 sts wide and 3 sts high.

Rnds 1-3: *3 sc with MC, 3 sc with CC; rep from * around and end with 1 sl st into 1st sc.

Rnds 4-6: *3 sc with CC, 3 sc with MC; rep from * around and end with 1 sl st into 1st sc.

Rnds 7-9: Work as for Rnds 1-3.

Work another 5 rnds in sc with MC, ending with 1 rnd CC.

FINISHING

Weave in all ends neatly on WS. Lightly steam press hat on WS under a damp pressing cloth.

Summer Bag

A cool bag as nice for city walks as on the beach. This design is timeless and one to keep using for many years.

FINISHED MEASUREMENTS
Length: approx. 12¾ in / 32 cm
Width: approx. 21¼ in / 54 cm
Handles: 13½ in / 34 cm long and 1¼ in / 3 cm wide

MATERIALS
Yarn: (CYCA #4), Rowan Summer Tweed (70% silk, 30% cotton; 131 yd/120 m / 50 g)
Yarn Amounts: 2 balls each Denim Blue #529, Tonic #551, and Bamboo #552
Hook: U.S. sizes G-6 and 7 / 4 and 4.5 mm
Notions: 4 large snaps (can be omitted)

GAUGE
16 sts and 9 rows (approx. 3½ shells wide and 5 shells high) in pattern with larger hook = 4 x 4 in / 10 x 10 cm.
16 sts and 20 rows in sc with smaller hook = 4 x 4 in / 10 x 10 cm.
Adjust hook sizes to obtain correct gauge if necessary.

PATTERN
Fans: see page 45.
Stripes: 2 rows Denim Blue, 2 rows Tonic, 2 rows Bamboo.
Repeat these 6 rows.

BACK and FRONT (make both alike)
First side: With larger hook, ch 80 and work in fan pattern and color stripes for a total of 22 rows. Continue stripes and dec ½ fan on each side on every row until 11 fans rem = 66 sts. Dec as follows: Sl st to the center dc of fan, 1 sc in dc, work in pattern to last fan and end row with 1 sc in the center dc; turn. Next, work 4 rows (= 2 stripes) without decreasing. Change to smaller hook and turquoise and work in sc, turning every row with ch 1. *At the same time*, dec on 1st row with sc 2 tog on each side of the center dc of every fan. Dec on the next row: *3 sc, 2 sc tog; rep from * to last 3 sts and end with 3 sc = approx. 32 sts rem. Work 2 rows in sc with Bamboo and then 2 rows sc with Tonic. Cut yarn and fasten off.
Second side: Begin at foundation ch, working into opposite side of chain. Work as for first side of bag.

FINISHING
Weave in all ends neatly on WS. Pin out bag to finished measurements and lightly spray with water. Leave until completely dry.
With RS facing, smaller hook, and Tonic, begin at foundation chain, crocheting around the sides of the bag as follows: Work 1 sc and 2 sc tog over each fan row up to the striped edge which is then worked with sc. There should be approx. 32 sts on a side. Work 6 sc to short side of the striped edge, ch 55 (one handle). Begin working the other side with 6 sc to short side of the striped edge, then 2 sc tog to fan pattern, ending at foundation chain. Work the opposite side the same way. Finish with 1 st st into the 1st st. Continue around in sc, beginning each row with ch 1 and ending with 1 sl st into 1st ch. Work another 2 rows Tonic, then 2 rows Bamboo, and 2 rows Tonic. Fasten off yarn ends. Sew on 2 large snaps at each side

below the handle if you think the bag hangs open too much.

TIPS & TRICKS
You can vary this bag is so many ways. If you want a deeper bag, make the straight section of the fan pattern longer before you begin decreasing. Sew the straight sides and only crochet the edging to the shaped section. This bag will also look good in one color, perhaps with a contrast color for the handles and edgings.
You can even line the bag and add an inner pocket.

The coolest bag!

Purple Scarf

This lovely scarf goes beautifully with the hat shown on page 126, even though the yarn and stitches are different. Color is the key—the hat's turquoise is echoed in the scarf.

FINISHED MEASUREMENTS
15 x 65 in / 38 x 165 cm

MATERIALS
Yarn: (CYCA #4), Colinette Mohair hand-dyed (73% mohair, 22% wool, 5% nylon; 102 yd/93 m / 50 g)
Yarn Amounts: 3 skeins Florentina
Hook: U.S. size J-10 / 6 mm

GAUGE
12 sts and 6 rows in dc pattern = 4 x 4 in / 10 x 10 cm.
Adjust hook size to obtain correct gauge if necessary.

Bobble: *Yarn around hook, work around the last dc, yo, bring yarn through, yo, and bring through 2 loops; rep from * 2 times more, yo, bring through all 4 loops. There will be 3 dc worked around the same st.

PATTERN
Row 1: Ch 3 (= 1 dc), skip 1st dc, work 1 dc in each st (= in each ch and each dc), ending row with 1 dc in the 3rd st of 4 ch; turn.
Row 2: Ch 3 (= 1 dc), skip 1st dc, 1 dc in next dc, *ch 3, 1 bobble (see above) around the dc just made, skip 2 sts, work 1 dc in next st; rep from * across, ending with 1 dc in the top of tch; turn.
Row 3: Ch 3 (= 1 dc), 1 dc between 1st dc and 1st bobble, *ch 3, 1 bobble around previous dc, 1 dc between the next 2 bobbles; rep from * across, ending with 1 dc in the top of tch; turn.
Row 4: Work as for Row 3.
Row 5: Ch 5 (= 1 dc + ch 2), 1 dc between the 1st and 2nd bobbles, *ch 2, 1 dc between the next 2 bobbles; rep from * across, ending with 1 dc in top of tch; turn.
Row 6: Ch 3 (= 1 dc), skip 1st dc, *work 2 dc into next ch loop, 1 dc in next dc; rep from * across, ending with 1 dc in 3rd of the 5 ch; turn.
Row 7: Ch 4 (= 1 dc + ch 1), skip the 1st 2 dc, work 1 dc in next dc *ch 1, skip 1 dc, work 1 dc in next dc; rep from * across, ending with 1 dc in the top of tch; turn.
Repeat these 7 rows for pattern.

INSTRUCTIONS
The scarf is worked alternately in Net Blocks with ch 1 loop in between (see page 51) and pattern above.
Ch 52 and begin with foundation row: 1 dc in the 6th ch from hook, *ch 1, skip 1 ch, work 1 dc in next ch; rep from * across = 24 ch loops.
Continue with *6 rows dc blocks and 7 rows in pattern. Rep from * 8 times and end with 6 rows dc blocks. Cut yarn and fasten off.

FINISHING

Weave in yarn ends neatly on WS. Block scarf to finished measurements and
cover with a damp towel, or spray with water. Leave until completely dry.

Scarf with Inlay Strands

Crocheting with larger hooks is fun and fast. This simple scarf is greatly enhanced with contrast color inlay strands.

FINISHED MEASUREMENTS
13 x 65 in / 33 x 165 cm

MATERIALS
Yarn: (CYCA #4), Colinette Mohair hand-dyed (73% mohair, 22% wool, 5% nylon; 102 yd/93 m / 50 g)
Yarn Amounts: 3 skeins Nutmeg and 1 skein October Afternoon
Hook: U.S. size J-10 / 6 mm

GAUGE
14 sts and 12 rows in pattern = 4 x 4 in / 10 x 10 cm.
Adjust hook size to obtain correct gauge if necessary.

FINISHING
Inlay: Cut 18 lengths of October Afternoon the same length as scarf + 11¾ in / 30 cm. Bundle groups of 3 and weave them in and out of the blocks down the length of the scarf as follows: Count in from one long side and weave in a bundle of 3 yarn ends in the 5th row, skip 3 blocks, weave in a bundle of 3 strands in the next row (see page 66). Leave the center 3 block rows empty and then weave in yarn bundles in the rows to each side of these. There should be a total of 6 rows with October Afternoon.
Cut 36 lengths of October Afternoon the same length as *width* of scarf + 11¾ in / 30 cm. Make bundles of 3 strands and weave in the yarn across the scarf. Count up from one short end and weave in a yarn bundle through the 6th row of blocks, skip 2 rows, weave in a bundle in the 3rd row, *skip 4 rows, weave in a bundle in next row, skip 3 rows, weave in a bundle in next row; rep from * once more. There should be a total of 6 rows with October Afternoon. Do likewise on the opposite end of scarf. Knot the lengths near the edges of the scarf so they will be locked in. Trim ends with approx. 2½ in / 6 cm fringe on the sides and approx. 4¾ in / 12 cm at the ends.
Block scarf to finished measurements and cover with a damp towel, or spray with water. Leave until completely dry.

This scarf can be made a little more elegant by using a yarn that matches the Nutmeg tone-on-tone instead of the October Afternoon.

Harlequin Block Bag

A bag that's both pretty and practical. It does require some crochet experience, so it isn't a project for a complete beginner. If you've crocheted before, though, you shouldn't have any problems.

FINISHED MEASUREMENTS
11¾ x 11¾ x 2½ in / 30 x 30 x 6 cm

MATERIALS
Yarn: (CYCA #4), Rowan All Seasons Cotton (60% cotton, 40% acrylic; 98 yd/90 m / 50 g)
Yarn Amounts: 6 balls Organic #178 (MC), 2 balls each of Tornado #235 and Bark #231 (CC)
Hook: U.S. size 7 / 4.5 mm

GAUGE
2½ blocks in width and 6 blocks in length in the harlequin pattern = 4 x 4 in / 10 x 10 cm.
20 sts and 18 rows in dc pattern = 4 x 4 in / 10 x 10 cm.
Adjust hook size to obtain correct gauge if necessary.

HARLEQUIN PATTERN
Multiple of 8 sts + 1.
3 or 6 dc worked together:
Work 3 or 6 dc in a row, keep last loops of each on hook, and then bring yarn through all loops on hook.
Foundation Row: 3 dc, ch 1, and 3 dc in the 5th ch from hook, skip 3 ch, 1 sc in next ch, *skip 3 ch, 3 dc, ch 1, and 3 dc in next ch, skip 3 ch, 1 sc in next ch; rep from * across; turn.
Row 1: Ch 3, skip 1st sc, work 3 dc tog over the next 3 sts, *ch 7, skip 1 ch, work 6 dc tog over the next 6 dc (skipping sc in center); rep from * across, ending with ch 7, skip 1 ch, 3 dc tog over the last 3 dc, 1 dc in last ch; turn.
Row 2: Ch 3, skip 1st dc, 3 dc in center of skipped 3 dc, *1 sc in ch 2 rows below (so that the ch-7 loop is drawn together), (3 dc, ch 1, 3 dc) in center of the skipped 6 dc; rep from * across, ending with 1 sc in ch 2 rows below, 3 dc in center of the 3 dc tog, 1 dc in 3rd ch; turn.
Row 3: Ch 4, skip 1st dc, *6 dc tog over the next 6 dc (skip sc in center), ch 7, skip 1 ch; rep from * across, ending last rep with 6 dc tog over the next 6 dc (skipping sc at center), ch 3, 1 sc in tch; turn.
Row 4: Ch 1, 1 sc in 1st sc, *(3 dc, ch 1, 3 dc) in center of the skipped 6 dc, 1 sc in ch 2 rows below (so that the ch-7 loop is drawn together); rep from * across, ending with 3 dc, ch 1 and 3 dc in center of the skipped 6 dc, 1 sc I ch; turn.
Repeat Rows 1-4.

BACK and FRONT (work both alike)
With MC, ch 74. Beginning in 2nd ch from hook, work 1 row sc. Change to harlequin pattern, working it in the following color sequence:
Rows 1-6: Organic.
Rows 7 and 8: Tornado.
Rows 9-10: Bark.
Rows 11 and 12: Tornado.
Rows 13-18: Organic.
Rows 19 and 20: Bark.
Rows 21 and 22: Tornado.
Rows 23 and 24: Bark.
Repeat Rows 1-12 once more. Finish with 2 rows Organic—the piece should now measure approx. 16½ in / 42 cm. Cut

yarn and fasten off.

FINISHING

Block pieces to finished measurements. Lay a damp towel over them, or spray them with water. Leave pieces until completely dry.
Sew bag together at bottom.

Side and shoulder straps:
With MC, ch 12. Beginning in 2nd ch from hook, work back and forth in sc (turning every row with ch 1) until strip is approx. 11 x 39½ x 11 in / 28 + 100 + 28 cm long = total of 61½ in / 156 cm.
Securely sew short sides of strip to bottom of bag, making sure that the center of the strip matches the seam line on bag. Sew the strip about 11 in / 28 cm up the sides of the bag. Do not sew the last 5½ in / 14 cm of the bag together; instead, fold the flap to outside.
Lightly steam press seams.

Four Potholders

After granny squares, the most common crocheted projects are potholders. Maybe these aren't as practical as contemporary potholders made with modern materials but these are much prettier.

FINISHED MEASUREMENTS
8¾ x 8¾ in / 22 x 22 cm

MATERIALS
Yarn: (CYCA #3), Rowan Handknit Cotton (100% cotton; 92 yd/84 m / 50 g)

Yarn Amounts: To make all of the potholders, you'll need 200 g Bleached #263 and 200 g Black #252 as well as small amounts of Gooseberry #219, Violet #353, Yacht #357, and Rosso #215, for the edgings. For one potholder, you'll need 50 g each Bleached and Black, plus a small amount of a contrast color for the edging.

Hook: U.S. size G-6 / 4 mm

GAUGE
20 sts and 22 rows in sc = 4 x 4 in / 10 x 10 cm. Adjust hook size to obtain correct gauge if necessary.

LARGE BLOCKS POTHOLDER
With Bleached, ch 41. Beginning in 2nd ch from hook, work 1 row sc = 40 sc. Turn every row with ch 1.

Row 1: Work 20 sc with Bleached, change to Black and work 20 sc.

Row 2: Work 20 sc with Black, change to Bleached and work 20 sc.

Repeat Rows 1 and 2 until you've worked 21 rows. Change colors so that Bleached replaces Black and vice versa.

Repeat Rows 1 and 2 until there are 42 rows total.

Hanging loop: With Bleached, ch 15 in one corner and attach with 1 sl st to corner. Work approx. 30 sc around loop.

Edging: With Bleached, work 1 rnd of sc around potholder with 3 sc in each corner to keep edging flat. Change to Violet and work 1 rnd sc with 3 sc in each corner st, ending at hanging loop. Turn with ch 1 and work back in picot: *1 sc in each of next 2 sts, ch 2; rep from * around, working 2 sc in each corner st. Cut yarn and fasten off.

large blocks potholder

angled stripes potholder

checkerboard potholder

grandmother's potholder

CHECKERBOARD POTHOLDER

With Bleached, ch 41. Beginning in 2nd ch from hook, work 1 row sc = 40 sc. Turn every row with ch 1.

Rows 1-10: *Sc 10 with Bleached, change to Black and work 10 sc (see page 67 for how to change colors). Catch unused color with each st as you work across. Rep from * once more = 4 blocks.

Rows 11-20: *Sc 10 with Black, change to Bleached and work 10 sc; rep from * once more. Repeat Rows 1-20 until piece is 4 blocks high.

Hanging loop: With Bleached, ch 15 in one corner and attach with 1 sl st to corner. Work approx. 30 sc around loop.

Edging: With Bleached, work 1 rnd of sc around potholder with 3 sc in each corner to keep edging flat. Change to Gooseberry and work 1 rnd sc with 3 sc in each corner st, ending at hanging loop. Turn with ch 1 and work back with 1 sc, ch 1 in every other st and 3 sc in each corner st. Cut yarn and fasten off.

GRANDMOTHER'S POTHOLDER

Work the first 2 rnds with Bleached and then work 2 rnds with Black; continue alternating 2 rnds each of Bleached and Black.

Block

With Bleached, begin at the center with ch 6; join into a ring with 1 sl st into 1st ch.

Rnd 1: Ch 1 (= 1st st), 2 sc around ring, ch 1, *3 sc around ring, ch 1; rep from * 2 more times and end with 1 sl st into 1st ch. Begin every rnd with ch 1 and end with 1 sl st to 1st ch.

Rnd 2: Beginning in corner, ch 1, 1 sc in corner ch, *3 sc, (1 sc, ch 1, 1 sc) in next corner; rep from * 3 more times, ending in last corner with 1 sc, ch 1, 1 sl st into 1st ch.

Rnd 3: Change to Black and begin in a corner. Ch 1, 1 sc in corner ch, *5 sc, (1 sc, ch 1, 1 sc) in corner ch; rep from * 3 more times, ending in last corner with 1 sc, ch 1, 1 sl st into 1st ch.

Continue working around as for Rnd 3, with 2 more sc on each side and rnd. End with 2 rnds Bleached when square is 8¼ x 8¼ in / 21 x 21 cm.

Hanging Loop and Edging:

Work as for Checkerboard Potholder but use Rosso instead of Gooseberry.

ANGLED STRIPES POTHOLDER

With Bleached, begin at the center with ch 15; join into a ring with 1 sl st into 1st ch. Work 30 sc around ring. 18 sc will be used for the hanging loop and the rem 12 sc begin the square. Work back and forth in sc in stripes of 2 rows Bleached, 2 rows Black. Begin by working over the 12 sc as follows: Ch 1, work 1 sc in each of the next 6 sts, ch 2 (corner), 1 sc in next 6 sc; turn with ch 1. Work in sc to corner, (1 sc, ch 2, 1 sc) in corner, sc to end of row.

On every row, there will be 1 more stitch on each side of the corner. Work a total of 19 stripes, ending with 2 rows Bleached.

Edging: With Yacht, work 1 row sc with 3 sc in each corner and then work 1 row picot edging, as for Large Blocks Potholder.

FINISHING

Weave in all ends neatly on WS. Steam press potholders, or spray with water, and leave until completely dry.

Bread Basket

Bread baskets, jewelry baskets, napkin baskets, a little basket for saving small things. Or crochet a red basket, fill it with beautiful Christmas tree balls, and use it as a Christmas decoration!

FINISHED MEASUREMENTS
10¼ x 8 in / 26 x 20 cm, 2½ in / 6 cm high

MATERIALS
Yarn: (CYCA #2), 100% cotton 12/6 rug warp (approx. 1558 yd/1425 m / 500 g) and 100% cotton twine or another hard twisted cotton yarn for the edging.
Yarn Amounts: approx. 75 g rug warp in lime-green and small amount of twine.
Hook: U.S. size E-4 / 3.5 mm

GAUGE
22 sts and 25 rows in sc = 4 x 4 in / 10 x 10 cm. Adjust hook size to obtain correct gauge if necessary.

NOTE The body of the basket is worked with yarn held doubled, while the edging is worked with a single strand.

Base: With lime-green, ch 61. Beginning in 2nd ch from hook, work sc across = 60 sc. Turn every row with ch 1. Work back and forth in sc until piece measures 8 in / 20 cm. Do not fasten off.
Sides: Crochet around all the sides in sc, working sc 2 tog at each corner on every rnd 7 times and then work 3 sc tog at each corner on every rnd 3 times. Work 1 rnd without decreasing and then change to the edging yarn/cord. Work 2 rnds sc.

FINISHING
Weave in all ends neatly on WS. Steam press the basket, pressing the corners extra carefully.

TIPS & TRICKS
It is easy to change the size of this basket. You can make a smaller base and then make the sides higher or make a square base instead of a rectangular one.

Gray Pillow

This pillow couldn't be cozier or more beautiful. Anyone can crochet this, even though it looks rather difficult.

FINISHED MEASUREMENTS
15¾ x 23¾ in / 40 x 60 cm

MATERIALS
Yarn: (CYCA #2), Borgs Vävgarner Tuna (100% wool; 339 yd/310 m / 100 g)
Yarn Amounts: 50 g each of light, medium, and dark gray, black, and natural white
Hook: U.S. size E-4 / 3.5 mm
Notions: Backing fabric—the same measurements as crocheted piece + seam allowances; pillow form, 17¾ x 25½ in / 45 x 65 cm; optional: 16 in / 40 cm long zipper

GAUGE
25 sts and 20 rows in pattern = 4 x 4 in / 10 x 10 cm.
Adjust hook size to obtain correct gauge if necessary.

A pillow you can make many versions of—just change the color combinations.

With light gray, ch 84. Beginning in 2nd ch from hook, work across in sc = 83 sc.

Now work in wave pattern as follows:
Row 1 (RS): With light gray, ch 3 (= 1 dc), 1 dc in next st, *5 sc, 5 dc; rep from * across, ending last rep with 3 dc; turn. = 81 sts.
Row 2: With light gray, ch 3 (= 1 dc), 2 dc, *5 sc, 5 dc; rep from * across, ending last rep with 3 dc.
Row 3: Change to natural white and begin stripes. Ch 2, complete row with hdc across.
Row 4: Change to dark gray. Ch 1 (= 1 sc), 2 sc, *5 dc, 5 sc; rep from * across, ending last rep with 3 sc.
Row 5: With dark gray, work as for Row 4.
Row 6: Change to white and work as for Row 3.
Row 7: Change to medium gray. Ch 3, 2 dc, *5 sc, 5 dc; rep from * across, ending last rep with 3 dc.
Rows 8 and 9: With medium gray, ch 1 and work in sc across.

Row 10: With medium gray, ch 3, 2 dc, *5 sc, 5 dc; rep from * across, ending last rep with 3 dc.
Rows 11-18: Repeat Rows 3-10, substituting black for white and light gray for dark gray.

Continue in pattern as set, working every other pattern repeat with white and dark gray and alternate patterns with black and light gray. Work in pattern until piece measures 23¾ in / 60 cm or desired length. End the stripe pattern as it was begun, with Rows 1 and 2 in light gray. Finish with 1 row sc.

FINISHING
Weave in all ends neatly on WS. Block pillow to finished measurements. Lay a damp towel over pillow top and leave until completely dry, or lightly steam press under a damp pressing cloth.
Sew the backing and crocheted pillow top together along 3 sides. Insert pillow form and then seam the 4th side, or sew zipper in along one short side.

Hot Pad

You have to crochet hot pads with yarn that can stand the heat, unless you want one just for decoration. We chose a heavy hemp yarn for ours; although it's a little tricky to crochet with, the results will be both safe and pretty.

FINISHED MEASUREMENTS
11¾ x 11¾ in / 30 x 30 cm

MATERIALS
Yarn: heavy hemp cord
Yarn Amounts: approx. 75 g for 1 hot pad
Hook: U.S. size M/N-13 / 9 mm

GAUGE
The gauge isn't important; the size will depend on how heavy the cord is.

Ch 6 and join into a ring with 1 sl st.

Rnd 1: Ch 3 (= 1 dc), work 15 dc around ring and then 1 sl st into top of 3 ch.

Rnd 2: Ch 5 (= 1 dc + ch 2), (1 dc in next st, ch 2) 15 times, 1 sl st into top of beg ch.

Rnd 3: 1sl st into 1st ch loop, ch 3 (= 1 dc), 2 dc in the 1st ch loop, ch 1, (3 dc in next ch loop, ch 1) 15 times, 1 sl st into top of beg ch.

Rnd 4: Sl st to 1st ch loop, ch 1, 1 sc into ch loop, ch 3, skip 3 dc, 1 sc into next ch loop, ch 6, skip 3 dc, *1 sc into next ch loop, (ch 3, skip 3 dc, 1 sc into next ch loop) 3 times, ch 6, skip 3 dc; rep from * 2 more times, (1 sc in next ch loop, ch 3, skip 3 dc) 2 times,1 sl st into 1st sc.

Rnd 5: Sl st to 1st ch loop, ch 3 (= 1 dc), 2 dc in 1st ch loop, *(5 dc, ch 2, 5 dc) in next corner ch loop, (3 dc in next ch loop) 3 times; rep from * 2 more times, (5 dc, ch 2, 5 dc) in next corner ch loop, (3 dc in next ch loop) 2 times, 1 sl st into top of beg ch.

Rnd 6: Work crab st (see page 71) around, with 3 sc in each corner st.

FINISHING
Cut cord and draw end through last st. Secure the end by threading it through the crab stitch edging for about 2 in / 5 cm.

Tea Cozy

You can even use this tea cozy for keeping eggs warm. Crochet it in colors to match your china for a coordinated table setting.

FINISHED MEASUREMENTS
Height: approx. 9¾ in / 25 cm
Width: 12¾ in / 32 cm

MATERIALS
Yarn: (CYCA #2), Rowan Cotton Glace (100% cotton; 125 yd/114 m / 50 g)
Yarn Amounts: 1 ball each of Dijon #739, Aqua #858, Blood Orange #445, Heather #828, and Black #727
Hook: U.S. size D-3 / 3 mm
Notions: Synthetic quilt batting; lining fabric, the same measurements as cozy + seam allowances

GAUGE
26 sts and 20 rows in pattern = 4 x 4 in / 10 x 10 cm.
Adjust hook size to obtain correct gauge if necessary.

PATTERN
Row 1 (RS): Ch 3 and 2 dc in 1st st, skip 2 sts, *1 sc in next st, skip 2 sts, 5 dc in next st, skip 2 sts; rep from * to last 3 sts, skip 2 sts, 3 dc in last st; turn.
Row 2: Ch 1, 1 sc in 1st st, ch 2, *1 sc in sc of previous row, ch 2, 1 sc in the 3rd (center) dc of previous row, ch 2; rep from * across, ending with 1 sc in last st; turn.
Row 3: Ch 1, 1 sc in 1st st, *5 dc in sc worked over sc of previous row, 1 sc in sc worked in the 3rd dc of previous row; rep from * across, ending with 1 sc in last st; turn.
Row 4: Ch 1, *1 sc in sc of previous row, ch 2, 1 sc in the 3rd (center) dc of previous row, ch 2; rep from * across, ending with 1 sc in last st; turn.
Repeat Rows 1-4 for pattern.

Work the pattern in the following color sequence:
Row 1: Blood Orange.
Rows 2, 4, and 6: Black.
Row 3: Heather.
Row 5: Aqua.
Row 7: Dijon.
Row 8: Black.

Repeat Rows 1-8.

TEA COZY
Make 2 pieces alike.
With Dijon, ch 98. Beginning in 2nd ch from hook, sc across. End every row with ch 1. Work total of 4 rows sc.
Change to pattern and color sequence until piece is a total of 8 in / 20 cm long.
Now shape top by working a half dc group less at each side: turn before the last 3 sts of every row until 48 sts rem. The piece should now measure approx. 9¾ in / 25 cm. Cut yarn and fasten off.

FINISHING
Weave in all ends neatly on WS by threading yarn in a short distance, turning, and threading back, so each yarn tail ends up at a seam line.
Top Loop: With Dijon, ch 26, work 1 row sc, change to Blood Orange, and work another 3 rows sc. End with 1 row Dijon. Cut yarn and fasten off.
Assembly: Block pieces. Lay a damp towel over pieces and leave until completely dry.

Cut the lining fabric and batting, following the outer edges of the cozy pieces + seam allowances. Seam the batting and then the lining. Trim cut edges. Trim the batting as close to the seam as possible.

Fold the top loop in half and sew end down securely to top of cozy. Seam the cozy pieces, rounding the top shaping at the same time. Insert the batting and then the lining. Baste with short stitches through all the layers so the pieces stay in place. Trim any excess batting, fold down the lining, and sew cozy together along lower edge.

Chevron Pattern Pillow

Pillows are like blankets and shawls—you can't have too many. In case you decide you do have too many, they make perfect gifts for good friends.

FINISHED MEASUREMENTS

17¼ x 14¼ in / 44 x 36 cm

MATERIALS

Yarn: (CYCA #2), Rowan Cotton Glace (100% cotton; 125 yd/114 m / 50 g)

Yarn Amounts: 50 g each of Shell #845, Rose #861, Blood Orange #445, Bleached #726, Ecru #725, Oyster #730, Mineral #856, Greengage #864, and Toffee #843

Hook: U.S. size E-4 / 3.5 mm

Notions: Backing fabric—the same measurements as crocheted piece + seam allowances; pillow form, 17¾ x 17¾ in / 45 x 45 cm, which will be adjusted for an oblong pillow

GAUGE

22 sts and 11 rows in pattern = approx. 4 x 4 in / 10 x 10 cm.
Adjust hook size to obtain correct gauge if necessary.

Instructions

With Shell, ch 83. The pattern is a multiple of 10 sts + 1 + 2 extra for tch.

Row 1: 1 dc in 3rd ch from hook, *3 dc, 3 dc tog, 3 dc, 3 dc in same st; rep from * across, ending with 2 dc in last ch.

Row 2: Ch 3, 1 dc in 1st dc, *3 dc, 3 dc tog, 3 dc, 3 dc in same st; rep from * across, ending with 2 dc in top of beg ch.

Repeat Row 2 throughout.

NOTE The Bleached rows are worked in sc instead of dc, but with the same pattern of increases and decreases.

Stripe Color Sequence

Rows 1-2: Shell.
Row 3: Rose.
Rows 4-5: Blood Orange.
Row 6: Bleached (work with sc instead of dc).
Row 7: Ecru.
Rows 8-9: Oyster.
Rows 10-11: Mineral.
Row 12: Greengage.
Rows 13-15: Toffee.
Row 16: Greengage.
Rows 17-18: Mineral.
Rows 19-20: Oyster.
Row 21: Ecru.
Row 22: Bleached (work with sc instead of dc).
Row 23: Rose.

Row 24: Blood Orange.
After completing Row 24, work backwards through sequence: Rows 23-1.

FINISHING

Weave in all ends neatly on WS. Block pillow top or carefully steam press under a damp pressing cloth.

Ruffled Edging: With natural white, work 3 dc in each row along one long side and then work back with 1 dc in each dc. Change to white and work 1 row sc. Work edging the same way along the other long side.

Back: Cut backing fabric to same measurements as pillow top + seam allowances. Sew backing to pillow top along 3 sides.

Pillow form: It is difficult to find oblong pillow forms but you can make your own. Shake the filling down to the bottom of the pillow and fold down one side about 4 in / 10 cm. Sew the fold in place with basting or back stitch. Insert pillow form and sew last side of cover together.

TIPS & TRICKS

This pattern also makes lovely placemats—or why not crochet a table runner, repeating the color sequence until the yarn runs out?

Large Granny Square Blanket

Usually granny square blankets are composed of many individual squares that are sewn together. Why not make one huge granny square that will become a blanket without sewing a single stitch?

FINISHED MEASUREMENTS
42½ x 42½ in / 108 x 108 cm

MATERIALS
Yarn: (CYCA #2), sportweight yarn (100% wool; approx. 339 yd/310 m / 100 g)

Yarn Amounts: 4 skeins white, 2 skeins yellow, 7 skeins light gray, 8 skeins dark gray, 15 skeins medium gray. These yarn amounts are not exact. We began with leftover tweed yarns but, as the blanket grew, we added weaving yarns in natural colors. This is a perfect project for anyone with a good stash of leftover yarns.

Hook: U.S. size E-4 / 3.5 mm

GAUGE
Gauge is not important for this project—simply crochet around until the blanket is the size you like.

BLANKET
Begin as for a regular granny square and keep working until blanket reaches desired dimensions.

With white, ch 6 and join into a ring with 1 sl st.

Rnd 1: Ch 3 (= 1st dc), 2 dc around chain ring, ch 3, (3 dc around chain ring, ch 3) 3 times, 1 sl st into top of beg ch.

Rnd 2: Ch 3, 2 dc, ch 3, 3 dc in corner loop, ch 1, (3 dc, ch 3, 3 dc in corner, ch 1) 3 times. Change color.

Rnd 3: Ch 3, 2 dc, ch 3, 3 dc in corner, *ch 1, 3 dc in ch, ch 1, (3 dc, ch 3, 3 dc) in corner; rep from * around. Change color.

Rnd 4: Ch 3, 2 dc, ch 3, 3 dc in corner, *ch 1, 3 dc in ch, ch 1, 3 dc in ch, ch 1, (3 dc, ch 3, 3 dc) in corner; rep from * around. Continue in granny square pattern, changing colors as you like. Here's the color sequence we used:

Rnds 5 and following: Work as for Rnd 4, increasing with another set of 3 dc on each side of every round.

COLOR SEQUENCE:
Rnd 1: White.
Rnd 2: Medium gray.
Rnd 3: Dark gray.
Rnds 4-7: White.
Rnd 8: Yellow.
Rnds 9-11: Medium gray.
Rnd 12: Dark gray.
Rnds 13-15: Medium gray.
Rnds 16-18: White.
Rnds 19-20: Medium gray.
Rnd 21: Yellow.
Rnd 22: Dark gray.
Rnds 23-25: Medium gray.
Rnd 26: White.
Rnds 27-28: Medium gray.
Rnd 29: Yellow.
Rnds 30-31: Dark gray.
Rnds 32-33: Medium gray.
Rnd 34: Dark gray.
Rnds 35-36: Medium gray.
Rnd 37: Yellow.
Rnd 38: Dark gray.
Rnds 39-40: Medium gray.
Rnd 41: Light gray.
Rnds 42-44: Dark gray.

Rnds 45-46: Medium gray.
Rnd 47: Light gray.
Rnds 48-49: Dark gray.
Rnds 50-51: Medium gray.
Rnds 52-53: Dark gray.
Rnd 54: Light gray.
Rnds 55-59: Medium gray.
Rnd 60: Light gray.
Rnd 61: Medium gray.

FINISHING

Weave in all ends neatly on WS. Block blanket to finished measurements. Lay a damp towel over it and leave until completely dry. You can also block blanket by lightly steam pressing it under a damp pressing cloth.

This blanket can be crocheted with leftover yarns in any color sequence you like.

Round Bolster Pillow

Round and oblong pillows are both pretty and practical. They are easy to throw into place and wonderful to nestle into after a long workday.

FINISHED MEASUREMENTS
Length: 16½ in / 42 cm
Diameter: 6 in / 15 cm

MATERIALS
Yarn: (CYCA #3), Rowan Creative Linen (50% linen, 50% cotton; 219 yd/200 m / 100 g)
Yarn Amounts: 100 g each of Natural #621, Denim #630, and Stormy #635
Hook: U.S. size G-6 / 4 mm
Notions: Pillow form, 15¾ in / 40 cm long and 6 in / 15 cm diameter; 2 shank buttons, approx. 2½ in / 6 cm diameter.

GAUGE
16 sts and 25 rows in pattern = approx. 4 x 4 in / 10 x 10 cm.
Adjust hook size to obtain correct gauge if necessary.

CENTER
Stripe sequence: *4 rows Natural, 4 rows Denim, 4 rows Stormy; rep from * throughout. The pattern used is Deep Spike Single Crochet (see page 64), changing colors after every 4th row.
With Natural, ch 77. Work in Deep Spike Single Crochet, changing colors following the sequence above. Work in pattern until piece measures approx. 16½ in / 42 cm, ending with 4 rows Natural.

SHORT ENDS (make 2 alike)
The ends are double crochet circles. Working with Natural, begin with a ring (see page 13):

Ch 3, join and work 15 dc in ring and 1 sl st into top of beg ch.
Rnd 1: Ch 3, 1 dc at base of the ch-3, 2 dc in each dc around, 1 sl st into top of beg ch = 32 sts.
Rnd 2: Ch 3, 1 dc in base of the ch-3, *1 dc, 2 dc in next st; rep from * around, ending with 1 sl st into top of beg ch = 48 sts.
Continue as set for a total of 6 rnds, with 1 more dc between each inc on every rnd. The circle should be approx. 6 in / 15 cm diameter.

FINISHING
Weave in all ends neatly on WS. Block pillow to finished measurements. Lay a damp towel over pillow pieces and leave until completely dry. With WS facing, seam the center piece to form a tube. Leave a small section open at the center so you can insert the pillow form.
Make 2 button covers with Denim (2½ in / 6 cm diameter)—see page 72. Sew one button to the center of each end piece. With WS facing, pin the ends to the tube and sew in ends.
Turn the tube right side out. Insert pillow form and seam opening.

Large Round Pillow

Two contrasting colors on a large pillow can really make a room. This pillow works equally well on a bed or as soft, extra back support on a chair.

FINISHED MEASUREMENTS
Diameter: 19¾ in / 50 cm

MATERIALS
Yarn: (CYCA #6), Rowan Big Wool (100% Merino wool; 87 yd/80 m / 100 g)
Yarn Amounts: 200 g Lipstick #063 and 100 g Concrete #061
Hook: U.S. size M/N13 / 9 mm
Notions: It is difficult to find round pillow forms. Use a square form and round it out as follows: Draw a circle on the form, shake the filling away from the corners, fold in the corners, and hand- or machine-stitch the edges around the drawn circle.

GAUGE
9 sts and 4.5 rows in dc = approx. 4 x 4 in / 10 x 10 cm.
Adjust hook size to obtain correct gauge if necessary.

PILLOW (make 2 pieces alike)
With Concrete, ch 6. Join into a ring with 1 sl st.
NOTE Begin all rnds with ch 3 and end with 1 sl st into top of beg ch.
Rnd 1: Ch 3 (= 1st dc), work 11 dc around ring = 12 dc, end with 1 sl st into top of beg ch.
Rnd 2: Ch 3, 1 dc in the same st, *2 dc in next st; rep from * around and end with 1 sl st into top of beg ch = 24 sts.
Rnd 3: Ch 3, 1 dc in 1st st, 1 dc in next st, *2 dc in next st, 1 dc in next st; rep from * around and end with 1 sl st in top of beg ch = 36 sts.
Rnd 4: Ch 3, 1 dc in 1st st, 2 dc, *2 dc in next st, 1 dc each in next 2 sts; rep from * around and end with 1 sl st in top of beg ch = 48 sts.

Rnds 5-12: Work as for Rnd 3 with 1 dc more between each inc on every rnd. Change to Lipstick after Rnd 6.

FINISHING
Weave in all ends neatly on WS. Block the two circles. Lay a damp towel over them and leave until completely dry. Place the pieces with WS facing WS and crochet them together with Concrete, working 1 sc in each st around. Insert pillow form before you finish crocheting the pieces together.

Round Rug

Lots of people think that crocheting around and around is the most fun technique of all. Crocheting a rug with leftover yarns is ideal and you can use any colors in any sequence you like. The rug will be pretty no matter what you do.

FINISHED MEASUREMENTS
Diameter: 39½ in / 100 cm

MATERIALS
Yarn: (CYCA#2), Borgs Vävgarner Tuna (100% wool; 339 yd/310 m / 100 g)

Yarn Amounts: Since this rug is a project using leftover yarns, it is difficult to give a precise yarn amount. The colors and amounts we used were approx. 200 g each of red, cerise, and raspberry, and 100 g each of yellow, turquoise, white, and lime-green

Hook: U.S. size J-10 / 6 mm

GAUGE

16 sts and 18 rnds in sc with yarn held double = approx. 4 x 4 in / 10 x 10 cm.

Adjust hook size to obtain correct gauge if necessary.

NOTE Hold yarn double throughout.

Ch 4 and join into a ring with 1 sl st.

Begin with ch 1, 5 sc around ring, ending with 1 sl st to 1st ch = 6 sts. Begin the next rnd with ch 1 and 2 sc in each st around, ending with 1 sl st to 1st ch. Place marker in the 1st st so you can see where the rnd begins. Continue as set with each rnd, beginning with ch 1 and ending with 1 sl st to 1st ch. Increase on every rnd with 1 st more between increases each rnd. So, for example on the next rnd, work 1 sc between each inc and then 2 sc between increases on the following rnd, etc. However, do not stack increases, because that will give the rug straight rather than rounded edges between increases. Instead, stagger the increases by a couple of stitches on each rnd. Change colors as you like. Weave in or catch the yarn ends as you work so there won't be a lot of work later. We crocheted 1-3 rnds with shades of red and cerise and then single rnds of yellow, turquoise, white and lime-green. If you are using leftover yarns, use the ones you have least of first so there will be enough for a complete rnd. The outermost rnds take more yarn than you might think.

FINISHING
Edging: *Work 4 sc, ch 3, 1 sl st into 1st ch, insert hook into next st, rep from * around. Cut yarn and fasten off.

Blocking: Spread out the rug with a damp towel over it and steam press lightly, or spray rug with water, and leave until completely dry.

A round rug easily fits in anywhere.

Colorful Pillows

These bold pillows fit in well with modern furnishings. If you want more subtle styling, crochet them in a single color, with the narrow stripes in a matching color.

FINISHED MEASUREMENTS
18½ x 18½ in / 47 x 47 cm

MATERIALS
Yarn: (CYCA #2), Borgs Vävgarner Tuna (100% wool; 339 yd/310 m / 100 g)—yarn is held double throughout.

Yarn Amounts for Pillow in Red, Cerise, and Orange: 100 g each cerise, raspberry, orange, and red + small amounts turquoise, yellow, green, and purple

Yarn Amounts for Pillow in Purple, Turquoise, and Green: 100 g each purple, yellow, green, and turquoise + small amounts cerise, red, raspberry, and orange

Hook: U.S. size H-8 / 5 mm

Notions: Pillow form 20 x 20 in / 50 x 50 cm

GAUGE
The gauge varies by pattern and is not important. Crochet each pattern until yarn almost runs out, leaving some extra for the narrow stripes on the other pillow.

NOTE The pillows are worked with yarn held double with red/cerise/orange and purple/turquoise/green colorways.

PILLOW IN RED, CERISE, AND ORANGE
With yellow, ch 63. Beginning in 2nd ch from hook, work across in sc = 62 sc. Work 1 more row sc.

Change to orange and work relief stitch pattern, Front and Back Post Double Crochet Alternating Front and Back, (see page 62) until almost out of yarn, or approx. 9 in / 23 cm.

Change to green and work 2 rows sc.

Change to raspberry and work V-stitch Double Crochet (see page 42), until almost out of yarn, or approx. 9 in / 23 cm.

Change to purple and work 2 rows sc, making sure there are 62 sts across.

Change to red and work Groups with 2 and 3 V-stitch dc (see page 42), continuing until almost out of yarn, or approx. 10¼ in / 26 cm.

Change to turquoise and work 2 rows sc, decreasing 1 st on the 2nd row = 61 sts rem (so you have the correct stitch count for the next pattern).

Change to cerise and work Double Crochet and Half Fans (see page 47) until almost out of yarn, or approx. 9¾ in / 25 cm.

Change to yellow and work 2 rows sc. Cut yarn and fasten off. Fold the pillow at the center, with the RS facing out and the yellow bands matching. With yellow yarn, crochet the pillow together along the yellow bands, working 1 row sc through both first and last rows.

FINISHING
Weave in all ends neatly on WS. Block pillow, laying a damp towel over it or spraying with water. Leave until completely dry. Seam one side, insert pillow form, and seam opposite side.

TIPS & TRICKS
If the white fabric covering the pillow form shows through, make a casing for it with fabric matching one of the crochet pattern colors.

If you are making both pillows, save a little of each large pattern

color to use for the narrow bands on the other pillow.

PILLOW IN PURPLE, TURQUOISE, AND GREEN

Work as for the first pillow in the following colors and patterns:

Narrow Band 1
Raspberry.

Pattern Panel 1
Turquoise and pattern as follows:

Row 1: Dc across.
Row 2: Sc across.
Repeat Rows 1 and 2.

Narrow Band 2
Orange.

Pattern Panel 2
Green, worked in Fan pattern (see page 45).

Narrow Band 3
Cerise.

Pattern Panel 3
Yellow, inc/dec as necessary to stitch count of 61 and work Double Crochet and Half Fans pattern (see page 47).

Narrow Band 4
Red.

Pattern Panel 4
Purple, worked in V-stitch Double Crochet (see page 42).

Narrow Band 5
Raspberry.

Crocheted Containers

STRIPED CONTAINER

FINISHED MEASUREMENTS
Diameter: approx. 4¼ in / 11 cm
Height: 3½ in / 9 cm

MATERIALS
Yarn: (CYCA #2), 2-ply 100% linen yarn (approx. 284 yd/260 m / skein)
Yarn Amounts: Small amounts each of natural colors and white
Hook: U.S. size E-4 / 3.5 mm

GAUGE
20 sts and 18 rows in sc = approx. 4 x 4 in / 10 x 10 cm.
Adjust hook size to obtain correct gauge if necessary.

FAN CONTAINER

FINISHED MEASUREMENTS
Diameter: approx. 2½ in / 6 cm
Height: 2¾ in / 7 cm

MATERIALS
Yarn: (CYCA #2), 2-ply 100% cotton cord (approx. 43 yd/40 m / small skein)
Yarn Amounts: 1 skein natural and a small amount of contrast color
Hook: U.S. size E-4 / 3.5 mm

GAUGE
20 sts and 20 rows in sc = approx. 4 x 4 in / 10 x 10 cm.
Adjust hook size to obtain correct gauge if necessary.

These containers, nicely decorative on their own, are also practical for saving those small things that often create a mess.

STRIPED CONTAINER
Base
With natural color yarn, ch 4 and join into a ring with 1 sl st to 1st ch.
Foundation Rnd: Work 8 sc around ring.
NOTE End every rnd with 1 sl st into 1st sc. Begin every rnd in the 1st st after the sc joined with sl st on previous rnd. Place a marker in the 1st st so it is easier to see where the rnd begins.
Rnd 1: Work 2 sc in each st around = 16 sc.
Rnd 2: Work 2 sc in 1st st, 1 sc in next st; continue around alternating 2 sc in 1 st and 1 sc in next st = 24 sc.
Rnd 3: Work 2 sc in 1st st, 1 sc each in next 2 sts; continue, increasing in every 3rd st = 32 sc.
Continue, increasing as set with 1 st more between increases on each rnd until there are 7 sts between increases = 72 sc. Stack increases from rnd to rnd. There are 8 increases on each round.

Sides
Work around in sc through back loops only without increasing. Begin with 2 rnds natural, change to white and work 2 rnds and then continue in stripes of 2 rnds each natural and white until side is approx. 3½ in / 9 cm high. End with 2 rnds natural and then cut yarn and fasten off.

TIPS & TRICKS
You can easily make the container higher and wider. Crochet the base until it is desired diameter before starting the sides. Vary the striping on the sides as you like. You can make a lid by crocheting a circle slightly larger than the base of the container and then crocheting the side of the lid to desired depth.

FAN CONTAINER
Base
Ch 4 and join into a ring with 1 sl st in 1st ch.
Foundation Rnd: Work 8 sc around ring.

NOTE End every rnd with 1 sl st into 1st sc. Begin every rnd in the 1st st after the sc joined with sl st on previous rnd. Place a marker in the 1st st so it is easier to see where the rnd begins.

Rnd 1: Work 2 sc in each st around = 16 sc.

Rnd 2: Work 2 sc in 1st st, 1 sc in next st; continue around alternating 2 sc in 1 st and 1 sc in next st = 24 sc.

Rnds 3-4: Sc around, increasing 9 sts evenly spaced around = 42 sc.

Rnd 5: Work 1 sc in each st around, working loosely.

Sides

Continue around without increasing. Work in pattern below. The first rnd is worked into back loops of slip st rnd below to make a little ridge around the base.

Rnd 1: Ch 1, *1 sc in back loop of next st, skip 2 sts, 5 dc in back loop of next st (= shell), skip 2 sc. Rep from * around, ending with 1 sl st into 1st sc = 7 shells.

Rnd 2: Ch 3, 2 dc in sl st, *1 sc in center dc of next fan, work fan into next sc; rep from * around, ending with 2 dc in the same st as the 2 dc at beg of rnd, 1 sl st in top of beg ch.

Rnd 3: Ch 1, 1 sc in same st as sl st, *1 shell in next sc, 1 sc in center dc of next shell; rep from * around, ending with 1 sl st into 1st sc.

Repeat Rnds 2-3 until sides are 2½ in / 6 cm high. Work 1 rnd sc with contrast color. Cut yarn and fasten off.

TIPS & TRICKS

This little container makes a nice glass or mug holder, too.

Index